TO
Selena,
WITH LOVE

TO
Selena,
WITH LOVE

CHRIS PEREZ

A CELEBRA BOOK

Celebra
Published by the Penguin Group
Penguin Group (USA) LLC, 375 Hudson Street,
New York, New York 10014

USA | Canada | UK } Ireland | Australia | New Zealand | India | South Africa | China
penguin.com
A Penguin Random House Company

Published by Celebra, a division of Penguin Group (USA) LLC. Previously published in a Celebra
hardcover edition.

First Celebra Trade Paperback Printing, November 2013

CELEBRA TRADE PAPERBACK ISBN: 978-0-451-41406-9

THE LIBRARY OF CONGRESS HAS CATALOGED THE HARDCOVER EDITION OF THIS TITLE AS FOLLOWS:
Perez, Chris.
To Selena, with Love/Chris Perez.
p. cm.
ISBN 978-0-451-41404-5
1. Selena, 1971–1995. 2. Singers—United States—Biography.
3. Mexican-American women singers—Biography. 4. Perez, Chris.
5. Tejano musicians—Biography. I. Title.
ML420.S458P47 2012
782.42164092—dc23 2011046126
[B]

Printed in the United States of America
33rd Printing

Set in Carre Noir STD
Designed by Alissa Amell

PUBLISHER'S NOTE
Penguin is committed to publishing works of quality and integrity. In that spirit, we are proud to offer
this book to our readers; however the story, the experiences and the words are the author's alone..

To the loving memory of Selena Quintanilla Perez and her dedicated fans around the world.

I can't erase this lonely heart that keeps on remembering.
Every day I live, I live with you, and with all the
things we'll never do.
Heaven holds a place for souls like mine.
Try to leave my troubled past behind.
You know it's so damn hard letting go . . .
Standing here, holding my heart in my hands
Yes, I am . . .
Trying to live every day the best I can.

—*Lyrics from "Best I Can," The Chris Perez Band*

PROLOGUE

A year after writing *To Selena, With Love*, I discovered an old letter from Selena. It was stashed in a little plastic bag with some photographs, but I immediately recognized the lined yellow paper she used to write on. The paper was folded, and on the outside she'd written, "*I love you*, Chris!" in her beautiful handwriting.

When I realized what it was, my heart started racing. I was with other people at the time, so I didn't want to read the letter right away. I knew the sight of Selena's words on the page would send me reeling back in time again.

I waited until I was alone that night before I finally unfolded those precious sheets of yellow paper. Selena had written the letter in late 1991 during a tough time in our relationship. I had been in Selena's band for a while and we had fallen in love. Then her father discovered our relationship and tried to banish me from the band— and from his daughter's life—forever.

Instead of being able to see each other nearly every day while we toured with the band, Selena and I now had to be apart most of the time. I was playing in two other bands on weekends and the two of us lived in different cities. Neither of us had cell phones back then, so we couldn't communicate easily or often. Selena was afraid I was falling out of love with her. That wasn't true, of course, but it was difficult to reassure her of my commitment when we hardly saw each other.

I was right about Selena's letter transporting me back to that place and time. It let me hear her voice clearly again as the letter took me back to that crazy year before we eloped. Here's what she wrote to me:

Hi Love,

What's up? Nothing much here. I'm just hanging around here thinking about you like always and of course wishing you were here right now. You know I could use one of your bear hugs right this very minute.

I just wish that you would talk or open up to me a little more, but I guess that it is my fault for always getting upset for something and I'm sorry babe. I guess sometimes I can be selfish and I realized that because I know that I'm used to getting what I want most of the time! Which is not too good cause I know that it's the same for you. I guess I just have to learn to be more mature about our relationship in order for it to grow stronger.

I'm sorry for freaking you out about wanting to get married, but I guess I'm feeling you out, trying to figure out . . . how much you love me. It's kinda stupid, but ever since you've been gone from the band and I don't talk to you as much cause of my phone being disconnected, I feel like you don't want me as much as I still want you! Does that make sense to you? It scares me that I'm gonna fight to be with you and in the end you are going to wind up telling me you no longer want to be with me and you've found someone new. It would devastate (I don't know if that's spelled right!) me if that were to happen. I know I couldn't handle it. I need you in my life Chris. I love you so much that it hurts for me to be apart from you. I can't run to you cause you're not here to hold me.

But I better let you go cause I'm gonna start crying again. But I do love you despite all the confusion I feel right now, so please bear with me, love . . .

Remember I'll always and forever love you and I miss you, more as every second goes by.

I love you always,
Selena

I had expected to relive my grief when I read the letter. But instead, my sorrow was mixed with joy and peace. I actually felt happy seeing Selena's words, because the letter let me have that part of her again that she once gave me. That's the moment I realized that writing this book, and having it be so generously received by Selena's fans, helped me reach a new level of peace in my life.

I first decided to write *To Selena, with Love* because grief had kept me from truly moving forward. I was putting one foot in front of the other without really progressing in my life. Once I finally started putting some of my memories on paper, I realized that I had boxes and boxes of baggage I hadn't dealt with after Selena's death. It was time for me to dust them off and sort through them.

I did this partly for myself, but also to show my gratitude to Selena's fans for all of the support they gave her, and our band, while she was alive. To her fans, it's clear that Selena wasn't just a talented, beautiful woman. She was a down-to-earth person who worked hard for her success in a male-dominated music industry.

When Selena hit the music scene, she started opening doors for other performers not just in Latin music, but in the mainstream world, too. Performers likes Jennifer Lopez, Shakira, and Beyoncé—who has talked about what it meant to her to meet Selena at the Galleria Mall in Houston when she was young—have all paid homage to Selena's influence.

I knew on some level how popular Selena was, of course, but when she passed away, the outpour of love and support we got from the fans stunned me. I wasn't prepared for that. Her fans have continued to keep Selena's memory alive and I am grateful to them for that. Now, by writing our story, I wanted to give something back to them. I hoped to shine a different light on Selena and show her fans who she really was offstage as a daughter, a friend, and a loving wife.

I also wanted to write this book as a way of setting straight some of the rumors flying around after her death. For instance, a lot of people had heard that Selena and I were having problems in our marriage. Others had heard she might have been pregnant when she died. In *To Selena, with Love*, I hoped to finally explain things in my own way and tell the truth as I lived it.

I was nervous during the process of getting the words down on paper, but ultimately, by the time the book was ready for publication, I felt satisfied that I had treated Selena—and her family—with the respect and dignity they deserved. I hoped Selena's fans would feel the same way, but I couldn't be sure.

My first book signing was held at a Barnes & Noble bookstore in Houston, Texas. I was shocked not only by the presence of so many fans—the line literally went out the door and around the corner—but by their generous comments about the book and the passion they obviously still felt for Selena and her music.

As I promoted the book over the next year, I was surprised and touched over and over again by the loyalty of Selena's fans. Sometimes we'd pull into a city and pass a building with a big line in front of it, and I'd say, "Wow, what's going on over there?" only to be told that the line was made up of people waiting for me to sign their books. I remember one supermarket in Laredo, Texas, where I was supposed to sign books for two hours, but it took me five. The supermarket staff was wonderful, handing out bottles of water to the people waiting in the sun. I made sure to get to the last person in line. If Selena's fans were going to show that kind of love, it was the least I could do.

It was always worth it, too. Many people would come up to me and break down in tears, saying how much they missed her. It felt good to share those moments with them, hugging them and thanking them for helping me remember Selena. Many thanked me, too, for offering them glimpses of the Selena they didn't know—the private Selena, the one who loved dogs and motorcycles and cooking, the woman who happily decorated her bedroom with an aquarium headboard but was terrified of snakes.

Even Selena's family has offered their support for this book, something I am extremely grateful to have. We went through a lot together.

Not long after the book was published, Selena's brother A.B. surprised me with a late-night phone call. It was weird, because I hadn't heard from him in a long time.

"Hey, what's going on?" A.B. said, just like we were still talking every day.

"Nothing. What's up with you?" I answered.

"I was just thinking of the old days and missing you," A.B. said. "I hope I get to see you soon."

"Yeah, me, too," I said, but I was still puzzled. Why would A.B. suddenly call me in the middle of the night?

He soon told me why as we kept talking: A.B. said he had been wandering around in a Walmart. "The next thing I know, I look up and there's your book on the shelf, so of course I had to pick it up and start reading it."

The book led us to have a nice heart-to-heart talk for the first time in what felt like forever.

Writing *To Selena, with Love* has propelled my life forward in so many positive ways. I feel like I'm finally finding a "new normal." Sharing my stories about Selena has given me a fresh sense of freedom to move on and concentrate on music. Selena and I first fell in love partly because of our shared love of music, so I know this is what Selena would have wanted me to do.

Currently I'm working on a CD of rock music in both Spanish and English with songwriter and producer Emilio Estefan, whose wife, Gloria, was one of Selena's biggest inspirations. We met Gloria and Emilio when we were first married and attended the same music awards, and I know Selena would approve of me working on this album. Emilio is such a hard worker and nice guy that he makes me want to be a better person, just like Selena did.

Selena and I often talked about having children together. Before being with her, I was young and selfish; my life was all about me. But Selena made me understand what joy there is in working hard to make the person you love happy. For instance, I had to learn to accept that Selena was always going to be pulled in many directions because she was juggling her father, her career, and her love for me. I constantly felt like I was walking on a fence and trying not to fall off on either side.

I was often thrust into things I didn't want any part of, like having to accompany Selena to interviews or photo shoots when nobody else wanted to go because we were all tired from traveling. For Selena, I would do it. All I had to do was look at her and watch how hard she worked, and I'd put a smile on my face and go. I knew it was the right thing to do because of how happy Selena was whenever I went with her; seeing her joy made me feel it, too.

I know I'm a better father because Selena taught me how to be generous in love. Today, my kids are a source of light and inspiration. My daughter, Cassie, now fourteen, recently chose to read *To Selena, with Love* for a school project. It was strange for me to see her reading it, of course, because even though she's a young lady who's growing up fast, Cassie will always be my baby. But I'm glad to share that part of my life with her.

Through social media, I've been able to continue communicating with Selena's fans long after I was finished with book signings. One of the most important ways I've been able to reach out is to support people who have written to me after reading the book because they've lost a wife or another family member. I've heard from people raw with grief because of losing loved ones to gun violence, accidents, domestic violence, and illnesses.

I remember one young fan in particular who contacted me on Facebook soon after the book first came out to ask how I kept going after Selena died. This girl was waiting at her high school for her boyfriend to pick her up so she wouldn't have to walk home alone. The next thing she knew, someone came to tell her he'd been shot. Her boyfriend was dead as a result of gang violence.

"How do you move forward?" she asked me. "I'm having trouble dealing with this."

What could I tell her?

Only the truth. Because of what I went through, I know how difficult it is to lose someone you love. "Give yourself time," I said. "You're going to grieve and go through your ups and downs. Grief never completely goes away, but it eventually becomes a part of you instead of controlling your life."

That message struck home once again when Jenni Rivera—a dear friend—was killed in a tragic plane accident in Mexico. Just before she died, I had gone to a studio in Los Angeles to record a song for her upcoming movie, *Filly Brown*, about a girl who wants to be a rap artist. Jenni played the girl's mother, who is trying to make amends for her mistakes from behind bars.

Like Selena, Jenni was more than just a talented singer. She was an amazing inspiration to millions of people because of the way she lived her life so generously out in the open, serving as a role model for many, many fans.

When I first got the phone call saying Jenni had died in a plane crash, it was a little bit like when everything happened with Selena. I didn't want to believe the rumors. I kept saying, "Hell, no. Don't tell me something this stupid." Despite the fact that I already knew from my own life that people die in tragic ways, I wasn't prepared for another loss.

When you're a child and you first start hearing about people dying in accidents or being murdered, it seems like it could never happen to you or to anybody you know. As you get older, though, you realize that death, whether it's sudden and tragic or expected after a long illness, happens to all of us. It is always a loss. You can't predict your fate or control what happens. The real gift lies in being able to appreciate the love you have, while you have it, knowing we only have a short time on earth before we must say good-bye.

If a fortune-teller had told me, back when I was twenty years old, that falling in love with Selena would end in me losing her the way I did, would I still have married her? Absolutely. For as long as I live, the day Selena died, March 31, 1995, will always be a painful day.

But I would do it all over again in a heartbeat. For Selena.

TO

Selena,

WITH LOVE

A month before she was murdered, Selena and I drove out to the property we'd bought in Corpus Christi. It was a beautiful piece of land, with a creek bordering one side and a hill that seemed to be the perfect place for us to build a house for the family we were planning. We loved driving out there at sunset and imagining our future together. Selena always told me that she wanted five kids, which made me laugh.

"Let's try having one baby first," I'd tell her. "Then we'll talk."

This particular evening, Selena and I sat on top of our hill watching the wide Texas sky turn every color from pale blue to bright peach to inky purple. "I want to raise our kids around lots of animals," Selena said. "Every kind of animal there is."

"You can't put all kinds of animals together," I teased. "You do that, you'll come outside and find nothing but a mound of feathers where something ate your chickens."

Selena leaned her head on my shoulder. "Just think, Chris. This is where our kids are going to be running around and playing someday soon. Can you believe it?"

I could, I told her. We continued to sit there until nearly dark, even though what I really wanted to do was jump up and start clearing our property right away. I didn't want there to be any coyotes or rattlesnakes around to bite our kids. I wanted to protect my family.

It didn't turn out that way, of course. I wasn't able to protect Selena.

After Selena was killed, I sold the property we owned together. I couldn't bear the thought of living on that land without her. I couldn't bear a lot of things for a while.

Lots of people asked me to write our story after Selena passed. I always said no. My feelings were too private. When we lose people who are precious to us, we all have to grieve in our own ways. My way was to keep my memories to myself. It was an automatic response for me to put a lid on my emotions after I lost Selena, because the feelings were so strong. I kept pushing my grief under the surface as I tried hard to continue what was left of my life.

I didn't want to think about Selena at all, because the sudden loss of everything we had worked for and believed in hurt too much. I thought about her anyway, of course. Every day, things would just enter my mind, uninvited. I'd hear one of Selena's songs on the radio, or see a story about her on TV, and the pain would surface again, sharp as a needle pricking the palm of your hand.

People kept asking me questions about her, too. They wanted to know why her father objected to me so strongly that Selena and I had to see each other secretly until finally, out of desperation, we eloped. They wanted to know whether Selena—who spoke regularly to schoolchildren about the importance of staying in school and staying off drugs—was as good and honest and generous as she acted in public—or was she just a really good actress? Did Selena have a dark secret? Was she murdered out of envy? Was her death the result of a drug deal gone wrong? Was she having a love affair? Was our marriage over?

I didn't care about setting the record straight at that point. I didn't answer any questions by the media or Selena's fans. I was too busy desperately trying to wall off that part of my life completely. I couldn't share my memories of Selena because that would mean accepting her death. I grieved in private and survived the loss by staying close to my family and continuing to play music. I even started a band and won my own Grammy for a Latin rock album called *Resurrection*, which featured songs that Selena inspired me to write after she was long gone.

Recently, though, I have begun to realize that, by burying everything, I've actually been living my life with blinders on, just putting one foot in front of the other without really moving forward at all. I started wondering if maybe I needed to remember everything after all, and if writing a book could help me finally come to terms with losing Selena.

Not long after I started having those thoughts, I got a phone call from my good friend Carlos. He was one of the few people I told about being in love with Selena back when she and I had to be so secretive about our relationship. It was a strange phone call at first. Carlos wasn't saying much, even though he was the one who'd called me. Finally I mentioned that I was thinking about writing a book.

"Man, that's so weird," Carlos said.

"Why? What's going on?" I asked.

"I had a dream about Selena last night. That's why I called you," he told me. "I was doing this show with my band in the dream and she came backstage. She was smiling, and she gave me a hug."

"That all sounds good," I said.

"Yeah, but the strange part is that at first I couldn't get any words out in the dream to talk to her," Carlos said. "Then Selena asked me how you were doing and I lost it. I told her you've been having a really hard time lately."

"Then what did she say?" I was picturing all of this just like it was happening in front of me.

"Selena gave me this big hug," Carlos said. "She told me not to worry about you. 'I got him,' she said, just like that."

I was quiet for a minute, feeling Selena close to me. Then I said, "I think it's time I wrote that book."

"Yeah," he said. "Selena would want you to do it."

So here it is: the story of my life with Selena. She deserves to be remembered not only for her beautiful voice and talent as an entertainer, but as a real woman who loved the ordinary everyday things, like walking barefoot in the evening to feel the warmth of the sidewalk on her skin.

Selena loved as hard as she lived. We loved her in return—her family, her friends, her fans, and me, her husband, who felt like the luckiest man alive every time Selena said my name. This book is for her.

ONE

HOLDING HANDS OVER MEXICO

Courtesy of Patricia Perez Ratcliff

*T*he seat next to me on the plane ride home from Acapulco was empty, but not for long. After a little while, Selena joined me. I had been playing guitar with Selena y Los Dinos for a year by then, but our journey together really began at that moment, as we started sharing our lives and falling in love while defying gravity in the bright blue cloudless sky over Mexico.

We started off with small talk, chatting about music and the trip we had just taken. Selena's brother, A.B., had treated me and some of the other band members to a vacation in Acapulco in exchange for writing a Coca-Cola jingle for Selena. Selena had started representing Coca-Cola even before I met her; we had written a jingle with a Tejano beat so that the Coke commercial would sound like a Selena song.

"Come to Mexico with us," A.B. had urged when I hesitated. "It'll be fun."

He was right. It was. It was also the trip that changed our lives forever.

Up until this point, Selena and I had always been friendly around each other, but professional. I was closer to her older sister,

Suzette, who played drums in the band and had a warm, wry sense of humor. With Suzette, I was comfortable enough to joke around, but I maintained a certain distance from Selena.

Selena was barely eighteen years old when I first joined her band, but she was already a seasoned professional entertainer. She had just signed with Capitol EMI, which was starting up its Latin division, and had a voice that went right to your heart.

Many singers hit the correct notes in a song. Still, they lack something. I don't really know how to explain what it is. Maybe they're singing a song like they're telling you a story, but they should be asking a question instead. Or they're growling when they should be purring.

Whatever a song required, Selena could do it all and still bring more. She was smart and picked up lyrics right away. More importantly, though, she had a musical range that went from a deep growl to a high soprano, and she could convey raw emotion with her voice, whether she was singing about love, loss, betrayal, or anger.

When Selena sang, it was always as if she sang directly to you. Everyone who heard her felt that. She had more stage presence and control over a crowd than anyone I'd ever met. It didn't hurt that she was beautiful and had a figure that could stop traffic.

When my guy friends found out that I was playing with Selena's band, they always teased me about her looks. The first thing out of their mouths was always something about how fine she was. I can't count how many times I heard them say, "Man, how lucky are you? You get to stand right behind her in the band and watch it all going on right there in front of your eyes!"

"Yeah, yeah," I'd say. "But the important thing is that she can *sing*."

Since joining the band, I hadn't had the chance to spend time alone with Selena. We were always in a group, whether we were onstage, on the bus, going out to eat if we were amped up after a show, in the studio, or playing video games.

Still, it didn't take me long to realize that Selena and I were polar opposites. She was lively and outgoing, and loved being the center of attention. Meanwhile, I quietly observed whatever was going on from the fringes, often just listening to music on my headphones or playing my guitar while everyone else fooled around. It didn't take Selena long to start joking about me being "too laid-back."

Sometimes I'd provoke Selena deliberately, just to tease her, and we quickly developed a little comedy routine around this. Selena would start talking while we were together with everyone, and I'd pretend that I wasn't paying any attention. I'd just keep staring ahead with my headphones on as if I could see right through her.

Selena would come stand right in front of me then and start moving her head from side to side, saying, "Hello? I'm right here!" If I could keep from laughing, she'd act like she was slapping me awake and I'd pretend to be startled. This got a laugh out of her every time.

Selena was always a lot of fun on tour. Besides joking around with me, she would pull pranks on the rest of the band members, challenge us to beat her at video games, or sneak food out of Suzette's hidden stashes of chips and cookies. It was only in Mexico, though, that Selena was truly free to be herself—and to act like an independent woman instead of everyone's kid sister.

You didn't have to be twenty-one to drink in Acapulco, so Selena and I were now able to go barhopping with the rest of the band. She'd stand shoulder to shoulder with me, leaning against me a little and talking excitedly about which restaurant we would go to

TO *Selena*, WITH LOVE

that night or what we might do with the others. Once, at dinner, we sat next to each other and I was conscious of her warm thigh pressing against mine. Of course I didn't complain about that.

On this vacation, beneath the swaying palm trees of Acapulco, I couldn't help but become increasingly aware of Selena's physical presence, her body enticing me even though she always wore cover-ups over her bikini. I tried not to stare at her, but I did anyway, watching her out of the corner of my eye when I thought she wasn't looking. A few times, I had caught her looking at me, too.

When we weren't on the beach, in the pool, or in the bars, we rented little boats on a cove and sped around. Selena was a daredevil, and she'd get hysterical every time we did this, laughing harder than I'd ever seen her let go. She had a great, contagious laugh, and pretty soon the rest of us would be hysterical, too.

Now that I was sitting so close to Selena on the plane, I was having trouble catching my breath. It was almost unbearable to sit there and not touch her. The air felt charged between us as Selena kept up the conversation, somehow managing to draw me out emotionally. I ended up telling her about how I first started playing music, my parents' divorce, and my dreams about becoming a rock musician—dreams I had temporarily set aside to play Tejano music.

Finally, Selena leaned a little closer and asked about my girlfriend back in San Antonio.

"She's fine, I guess," I answered. "Though I haven't talked to her since we left for Mexico."

After we had talked for a little while longer, Selena asked, "Would you look at something for me?" She reached into her purse and pulled out some proofs from a photo shoot she had done recently. "Tell me what you think of these," she said. "Be honest."

She handed me the pictures and I flipped through them. For the shoot, she'd dressed in a black bustier top and black tights, and she was standing on a beach. She looked amazing.

"You look incredible," I said. "You really do."

At that moment, the plane hit turbulence. I had never flown before this trip to Mexico, so the sudden jolt terrified me. I reacted by grabbing the armrest between our seats.

Selena laughed because I looked so scared. I laughed with her, but I was aware at the same time of feeling the side of her hand brush against mine. I wondered what would happen if I grabbed her hand. I thought it would probably either be a huge mistake—or the best idea ever.

And then we hit another bump, and Selena took my hand. As she assured me that everything would be all right, I forgot all about the turbulence. I probably even forgot that we were on a plane. I was too busy freaking out: I was happy, I was scared, and I didn't know what to do next. I just sat there with my fingers entwined with hers, hardly able to speak, my heart pounding.

Calm down, I told myself. Lots of friends hold hands. Selena took mine because I was scared. That's all it was: friends holding hands.

Selena must have read the emotions playing on my face, because when I dared to turn and look at her again, she said, "Is this okay? Are you cool with this?"

"Sure," I said. Meanwhile, I was dizzy, breathing in her scent, and inside I was screaming: *Yeah, it's cool!*

We sat there for the rest of the plane ride, talking and holding hands as if that were something we did every day. That was it. But something had changed between us.

13

When the plane landed, nobody seemed to have noticed anything. Or, if they did, they kept it to themselves. Selena and I hugged good-bye, and we did the same with everyone else. The rest of the band drove back to Corpus, but I went directly to my apartment in San Antonio, my girlfriend at the time, and my life as I knew it.

I was determined to discount everything that had happened on that flight home from Acapulco as a onetime thing. There was no point in getting involved with Selena, I reminded myself, because her protective father would never allow it. At the very least, it wouldn't be professional behavior on my part. At the very worst, I might lose my job.

However, as the days passed between my return from Acapulco and my next tour with Selena and the band, something started happening to me. I began to think about Selena constantly—her eyes, her lips, her body, her laughter—and feeling anxious to see her again. Part of me hoped that she felt the same way about me—while part of me hoped even more that she didn't, so that we could stay friends and keep playing music together.

The first time I heard Selena sing, it never crossed my mind that I would ever play in her band—much less that she would one day become my beloved wife.

I was playing guitar in a Tejano band fronted by another young singer, Shelly Lares. Even though Selena lived in Corpus Christi, about two hours from San Antonio, she and Shelly had become friends, partly because there were so few women in Tejano music at that time. One day, Shelly asked me to listen to Selena's new album, *Preciosa*, and tell her what I thought.

I looked at the album cover. *Great-looking girl*, I thought, studying her dark hair and warm brown eyes. I flipped the album over and saw a picture of the whole band, which included Selena's sister, Suzette, on drums and her brother, A.B., on bass. The musicians were young and dressed hip for the times, especially for a Tejano group.

"They're pretty cool looking," I told Shelly.

"She was just nominated for the 1988 Tejano female vocalist of the year," Shelly told me with a trace of envy. "Her brother was nominated for Tejano songwriter of the year."

Listening to the album, I knew instantly why Selena y Los Dinos were rising to the top in the Tejano world. Selena's voice was outstanding, and this group was adding unique sounds to traditional Tejano music.

Not that I was an expert. I was new to the Tejano world, and in fact I often felt like an imposter. I was a nineteen-year-old rock guitarist whose favorite groups included heavy metal bands like Mötley Crüe and Def Leppard. My initial reaction when my high school friend Tony Lares first tried to convince me to join his cousin Shelly's band was foot-dragging resistance.

Tejano music—a mix of traditional Mexican folk music, polkas, and country western sung in Spanish, sometimes with English lyrics mixed in—had been part of my childhood as a Mexican-American growing up in Texas, but it was the only kind of music that I seriously hated. When I was a little kid riding in the car with my grandmother, she'd put Tejano music on the radio and I'd be in the backseat covering my ears, shrieking, "Nooool!"

But Tony had caught me at a weak moment, and despite my dreams about running away to Los Angeles and starting a kick-ass rock band, I was sharing an apartment with my father and the only work I could find was shelving books at the local library. Tony's certainty that we could actually make money playing music—even if it was Tejano music at dances and weddings—convinced me to accept his offer.

Tony, Shelly, and the band schooled me in songs by Mazz, Laura Canales, David Lee Garza, La Mafia, and the Latin Breed—great Tejano groups that had emerged in the 1980s. When I first started playing with Shelly, I couldn't tell the difference between one group and the other. After a few months, though, I got so familiar with the music that I could tell in about four seconds of hearing something who was playing it. Tejano groups all had their individual sounds, just like musicians in any other genre.

At that time, Tejano music was like this big wave building, and we were all on surfboards. We didn't know just how big that wave was going to get, but we were all determined to ride it as far as we could.

The new musicians, especially those in Mazz and La Mafia, used powerful sound systems and staged their shows with flashy lights; they wore their hair long and dressed in spandex. Tejano music was transforming into something fresh; it certainly wasn't the same tired sounds that I used to hear in my grandmother's car. And Selena y Los Dinos were clearly unique. I knew as soon as I heard that album that they were pushing the envelope by fusing traditional Tejano music with rhythm and blues, Colombian cumbia, and pop.

As I listened to Selena y Los Dinos with Shelly, I read the credits on the album cover, shaking my head when I saw that Selena's brother, A. B. Quintanilla III, had not only arranged and produced this album, but had also written a lot of the songs. Selena had a beautiful voice, sure, but it was A.B. who first impressed me. I had become Shelly's musical director by default when Tony left the band; A.B. was doing what I fantasized about doing someday as a producer and songwriter.

"Wow," I told Shelly. "These guys are right in our backyard. I can't believe I've never gone to hear them."

"People are saying Selena y Los Dinos are going to sign a record deal with EMI Latin," Shelly said. "Want to come see them at my house? I have a videotape."

"Sure. Maybe we can cover some of their songs," I said.

That night, my friend Rudy Martinez, who played bass with our band, drove over to Shelly's house with me. We gathered around the television in the living room as Shelly inserted a tape into her VCR. The video was fuzzy—it had been shot with a camera on a tripod—but I could tell that Selena was already a showstopper. She had a cute figure, she could dance like no one else, and her voice was incredible. Even seeing Selena on this small screen, I felt her command of the stage. She had the audience standing up and dancing with her, and she worked the stage from one side to the other, exuding energy and charisma.

Even if I hadn't noticed Selena's looks myself, Rudy was determined to make me sit up and pay attention. Whenever he thought Shelly wasn't looking, Rudy would nudge me in the side with his elbow while we were on the sofa watching the tape.

"Check it out," he'd whisper.

"Yeah, I see her," I said.

"Oh, man," he said.

"I know," I said. But I wasn't really looking at Selena anymore. To me, she was just another entertainer. I was a lot more focused on watching the band and analyzing the instrumentals.

Afterward, Rudy and I drove home together. "Dude," Rudy said. "Did you see that?"

"Yeah, I saw it," I said, still deep in thought about the music. "Los Dinos sounded pretty good."

He laughed. "No, dude. The chick in the video. She was smokin' *hot*, man."

I laughed, too, never once imagining that, in only a few short months, I would be playing guitar in Selena's band—or that I had just seen my future wife on a VHS tape.

That Selena looked and sounded so comfortable onstage was only natural since she had been performing since childhood. Her father, Abraham Quintanilla, was a second-generation Mexican-American with musical aspirations of his own. In the early 1960s, he had sung with a doo-wop band called Los Dinos. Abraham and his group managed to get one hit on a Corpus Christi pop radio station, but when they couldn't break into the Top 40, Los Dinos turned to Tejano music and played in dance halls. Abraham eventually gave up music to support his wife, Marcella, and their children by working for the Dow Chemical Company in Lake Jackson, Texas.

The thing is, Abraham may have given up playing music, but he never stopped loving it. He may have been going to that chemical plant every day, but he still played his guitar at night after work. Selena would come and sit down to listen. By the time she was six years old, she was singing along—and Abraham recognized her talent immediately.

As a diversion for himself, mostly, Abraham decided to sound-proof the garage and form a family band. He taught Selena's older brother, A.B., to play the bass guitar. Abraham drafted Suzette, Selena's older sister, as the band's drummer—a move that Suzette fought constantly at first, because she thought it was too weird for a band to have a girl drummer. Abraham stuck to his mission, though, and pretty soon the family band was rehearsing for at least half an hour a day in that garage.

This hobby still wasn't enough to satisfy Abraham's creative urges entirely. When a friend told him that the town of Lake Jackson needed a good Mexican restaurant, he leased a space and started to serve authentic Mexican food—accompanied by Selena singing while A.B. and Suzette played their instruments. A.B. and Suzette were already in high school by then and were still resistant to the idea of playing Tejano music, especially since many of the kids they knew from school ate at their father's restaurant with their families. Selena didn't care. She was still just a nine-year-old kid having fun.

Business went well enough at the restaurant that Abraham decided to quit his job at Dow. Then, when the recession hit, he lost everything. Abraham had no luck finding another job in Corpus, so he turned to the only thing he knew: music. He named the family's band Selena y Los Dinos as an homage to his old band and took any paying gigs he could find between California and Florida: dance halls, ballrooms, skating rinks, VFW halls, you name it. Selena had to learn to sing in Spanish—which she didn't even speak. A.B. played the bass guitar and starting writing and arranging the band's songs. Suzette played drums and Abraham added in other musicians as needed.

Abraham supported the family partly by helping his younger brother Isaac run his trucking business. But, every weekend, he would load his family into a beat-up van, hook up a trailer for the equipment, and hit the road, playing any kind of show that would have them. At first they barely covered their expenses.

Gradually they started getting more shows, and Abraham was able to buy a bus—a '64 Eagle that the family dubbed "Big Bertha." The bus was in rough shape and had no heating, air-conditioning, restroom, running water, or power steering. In winter months, Selena and her family slept near the motor to stay warm; in the summer it was almost unbearable.

But their hard work paid off. By 1984, when Selena was barely thirteen years old, she had already recorded her first album with Los Dinos on the Freddie label. Abraham was so intent on having his family make it in the music business that he put those goals before nearly everything else. He was focused on seeing Selena's inevitable rise to stardom come to fruition.

By the time Selena was fifteen, she had appeared on the cover of *Tejano Entertainer* and was earning widespread notice as that genre's youngest female vocalist. She had released a major hit single, "*Dame un Beso*," written by A.B. and keyboardist Ricky Vela, followed in 1986 by another hit single, "A Million to One."

Despite knowing only a minimal amount of Spanish, Selena not only sang in that language, but had appeared twice on one of the most popular shows on Spanish-language television, the *Johnny Canales Show*, and performed in front of thousands of people in Matamoros, the Mexican border city.

In 1987, the year before I met her, Selena was crowned Female Entertainer of the Year at the Tejano Music Awards, knocking the previous queen of the scene, Laura Canales, right off her throne. Her father's instinct and drive had been on the mark—Selena y Los

Dinos had made six increasingly successful albums and she seemed unstoppable.

During that first year with Shelly Lares and her band, we did well. We were getting regular shows around San Antonio and we had even put out an album that featured three songs I cowrote with her. I was really getting into the game, going into the studio and recording with Shelly and acting as the band's musical director.

Now that I'd heard Selena y Los Dinos, we started covering their music and I became a serious fan of theirs. As much as I admired Selena's vocal abilities, however, I was still much more impressed by the stellar arrangements and production quality of Los Dinos, which I attributed to A.B. He was the band's bass player, and he was a good one, but it's no secret that the role of a bassist in almost any band is a supporting one; you have to lie down and hold the bottom end to give the other musicians the freedom to do what they do. A bass line has to be solid. It's like building a house: you can have the prettiest house on the block, but if the foundation isn't solid, the house will crack and fall.

Far more impressive than A.B.'s qualities as a musician were the intriguing ways he produced Selena y Los Dinos using the newest gear and most complex sounds I was hearing anywhere in Tejano music. I would hear one of their songs and say, "Oh, wow, what is that?"

For instance, A.B. was one of the first musicians to start incorporating the pop drum machine sounds that were being used by Top 40 English-language musicians like Janet Jackson or Paula Abdul at the time. I'd hear those sounds coming out of the speaker while playing an album by Selena y Los Dinos and feel confused but intrigued. This was supposed to be Tejano music—and most of the other Tejano groups were sticking to the traditional folk sounds created by accordions and drums. Even if A.B. did decide to incorporate an accordion sound, he would do it with an electronic keyboard. He was also on the cutting edge when it came to sequencing and sampling the mix on an album.

Later, after I joined Los Dinos and got to know everyone, I realized that A.B. was like the Wizard of Oz: he was behind the curtain, working the lights and levers, but in truth everyone in that band had enormous talent. It was a magical alchemy when they were all together. Until that time, though, the coolest thing I could imagine was to meet A.B. and ask him how he did what he did.

Amazingly, only a few months after first hearing *Preciosa*, I had my chance. We were in rehearsal one day when Shelly mentioned that Selena was playing in San Antonio that night. "We should go check her out," she suggested.

"Sure," I said, but I was in the middle of a song and didn't really think much about it. When I'm playing music, that's it—I'm focused on playing music and doing nothing else.

Toward the end of the day, however, the door to the studio opened and in came A.B. with several members of Los Dinos. They chatted with Shelly and her father. I wanted to join them, but I apologized and said that I was still wrapping things up with the band.

"Hey, no problem," A.B. said. "Don't mind us. We'll just watch. Y'all keep on playing."

I didn't know it then, but A.B. had actually come by the studio deliberately to scout me out. He was looking for a guitar player who could not only play traditional Tejano music, but help the band start covering more commercial rock and pop songs because their goal was to make a more mainstream English-language album one day.

I had been working that afternoon on a Pat Benatar song with Shelly's band. Now, with A.B. and his band members watching, we started the song again from the beginning.

After rehearsal, A.B. invited us to come hear Selena y Los Dinos play in the city, and that was the first time I saw Selena up onstage doing her thing. I didn't pay much attention to the singer. I was too busy watching A.B. and Los Dinos playing behind her and thinking, "They sound even better live!"

There were some other Tejano groups playing that night after Selena y Los Dinos, but they didn't interest me much. I went outside after a bit to get some fresh air and hang out with a group of friends. When I saw A.B. walking toward us, I broke away from the group and went to meet him.

"How did you like it?" he asked.

"It was incredible," I said.

And that's when A.B. told me that he had come by our rehearsal earlier that day specifically to see me on guitar. "I wanted to see if what I'd heard about your playing was true," he said.

"And?"

"I really liked what I heard."

I nodded, thanking him for the compliment, but I still didn't get what was coming until he dropped it on me: "What would you think about playing with Los Dinos?" he asked.

"I'd definitely be interested," I said. My heart was pounding hard; already I was imagining how much I could learn from playing music with someone as experienced and talented as A.B. seemed to be.

"Good," A.B. said. He scrawled his phone number on a piece of paper and handed it to me.

I was more than interested in joining Los Dinos—I was excited. But I had just started working with my friends Albert and Rudy in a new band, and I was conflicted about abandoning our project and being disloyal. I also knew that joining Los Dinos would mean staying with Tejano music instead of pursuing my dream of becoming a rock guitarist. Is that what I really wanted?

It was, I decided. I knew that I'd be playing at a whole new level if I could be with a group as sophisticated and hip sounding as Los Dinos.

A couple of days later, A.B. called and said, "Hey, do you want the gig with Los Dinos or not? We need you right now."

"I do," I hedged, "but I need to work some things out with the band I'm in now first."

The next day, I told Rudy about A.B.'s offer and how torn I was.

"What? He asked you to join Los Dinos?" Rudy said.

I nodded.

"Dude, what are you still doing with us, then?" Rudy asked.

"You mean if he'd asked you, you would have just jumped ship and left us?" I said, laughing.

"I'd already be gone," Rudy promised.

The next morning, I called A.B. and joined Los Dinos. That phone call set the course of my life in ways I never could have predicted.

But I guess that's always true in life, isn't it? You never know which decisions you make are going to be the big ones—even when they're as seemingly small as deciding to play a musical instrument or who to sit next to on a plane.

TWO

ROMANCE ON TOUR

About a month after our trip to Acapulco, Selena and I were talking alone in the darkened bunk area of the tour bus. I was lying in my bed, one of the upper bunks, and she was standing next to me, her elbow on the bunk. She was close enough for me to lean over and kiss her.

Suddenly, the door separating the bunks from the lounge area slapped open, making us both jump. Her father, Abraham, was supposed to be driving the bus. Instead, here he was, looming in the doorway and glaring at us.

Abraham didn't say a word. He looked at Selena, she looked at him, and then he walked on through the bunk area to the back of the bus.

Later, she told me that he asked her what we'd been doing. "Nothing," she had told him. "We were just talking."

"It didn't look like nothing," he said. "You don't want to make people think that something's going on between you and Chris."

Selena apologized and Abraham never said anything to me about it. To him, I was still a cool guy, a friend of the whole family. He thought that he could trust me with his daughter.

What he didn't know was that our feelings for each other had begun to build after that trip to Mexico, despite the constant scrutiny of Selena's parents and the other band members within the close quarters of the tour bus.

I hadn't meant for any of this to happen. As I boarded the tour bus for the first time after our trip to Acapulco, I had firmly reminded myself that becoming involved with Selena would bring nothing but trouble to both of us—and to Los Dinos as well. I was resolved not to let that happen.

The minute her luminous dark eyes met mine, however, I felt my defenses melt away. From then on, I decided to be open to anything that happened. My feelings for Selena were so overwhelming that I knew I had to give our relationship a one hundred percent chance.

Selena clearly felt the same way. Just as it had felt so natural to sit beside her on the plane from Mexico and hold hands while we talked, it felt natural now for us to spend as much time together as we could.

Before that trip to Mexico, I had kept a professional distance from her. Onstage, Selena sang up front while I was off in my own world, playing guitar and adjusting to this whole new life. Offstage, I saw her only with her family and other members of the band. Between gigs, I often stayed with A.B. when we were rehearsing or playing in Corpus, and sometimes Selena might join us to watch TV or talk for a little while, but that was it.

And that was the way it should be, I had thought during that first year I was with Los Dinos. Even if there had been sparks, I would have stomped them out because I knew that nothing could happen between us. I didn't want to jeopardize my job. I had a girlfriend in San Antonio. The last thing I needed was for some rumor to start up about us seeing each other.

At the very least, I knew that the Quintanilla family was tight, and Selena's father, Abraham—whom I liked and respected, and often kept company up front in the tour bus while he was driving—would feel furious and betrayed if he thought somebody in the band had the nerve to hit on his daughter.

That's why I had worked at maintaining distance from Selena and tried to think of her as a little sister. The only time I had ever wavered from this stance was a pure accident.

I was in Corpus with A.B. We were driving back from somewhere, and as we turned onto A.B.'s street, we saw a limo parked in front of his parents' house. The limo was for Suzette, Selena, and a group of their friends; they were all going together to a Garth Brooks concert. This was a big night for them and they were all dressed up.

Well, as we came around the corner, I spotted a woman with curly dark hair and an incredible body leaning into the window of the limo. I couldn't see her face.

"Oh, man, who's that?" I said to A.B.

A.B. started cracking up. "That's Selena, stupid," he said.

Of course, even if I had wanted to get closer to Selena, it would have been difficult. Abraham and Marcella, Selena's mother, were extremely protective of her. They had to be. On the Tejano music scene, stories were always flying about women entertainers getting stage time because they'd slept with so-and-so. It was important for Abraham to present his band, and especially his youngest daughter, as chaste and pure, no matter what costumes she wore onstage or how much makeup she wore.

Selena was therefore never without a chaperone. She and Suzette slept in their parents' hotel room when we were on the road, and Selena's parents accompanied her if she wasn't onstage, unless they sent A.B. or Suzette to chaperone her instead.

Even on the bus, Selena often sat in the back with her mother. Marcella and Selena could sit on the sofa back there and talk for hours. Sometimes Selena would lie with her head on her mom's lap, while Marcella played with Selena's hair or massaged her scalp. I'd walk back there sometimes and Selena would have this glazed look, like a cat. She was always Marcella's beloved baby girl.

After that fateful trip to Mexico, though, Selena and I started seeing each other secretly. Sometimes we'd just slip off to take a walk before one of the shows, or we might see a movie together or grab a bite to eat if we had a few hours to kill on the road. Abraham seemed cool with this; perhaps he thought it was natural for Selena and me to have a lot to talk about, since we were the youngest members of the band, and I'm sure he thought that Selena was safer in my company than she would have been out on the street by herself.

Meanwhile, Selena and I agreed that letting as few people as possible know about our feelings for one another was the best course of action, because then there would be less chance of anyone trying to tell us to put the brakes on. I didn't even let my closest friends in San Antonio know what was going on.

And, in a way, nothing really *was* going on, at least not physically. Onstage, it was business as usual. It was easy to act natural together despite our heightened awareness of one another, because Selena and I were so accustomed to playing together at that point. Offstage, we were always surrounded by her family, her fans, and the other band members. By the time I joined Los Dinos, the band also included keyboardist and songwriter Ricky Vela, and vocalist and songwriter Pete Astudillio. Pete was a Tejano star in his own right, whose duet with Selena in 1989, "Amame, Quiéreme," was nominated for Vocal Duo of the Year at the Tejano Music Awards soon after I joined the band.

Even though Selena and I were rarely alone, however, our feelings for each other rapidly grew and were soon so intense that I could almost imagine the air crackling with electricity whenever Selena walked into the room. We never touched, and yet I felt that something connected us—a force stronger than either of us.

There were plenty of reasons for me to fall in love with Selena. She was a talented, sensual dancer and singer, and a compelling entertainer. She really broke the mold in Tejano music with everything from the music she sang to the way she dressed in her glittery bustier tops and formfitting pants—later, a journalist would call her "the Mexican Madonna" partly because of her stage costumes. She was gorgeous, she was sexy, and she was also very funny.

I was attracted to that woman I saw onstage. But I fell in love with the real Selena, the woman who laughed hysterically while riding speedboats, was determined to beat every guy in the band at video games, and wore jeans and sneakers and a baseball hat on the bus. Selena had a huge talent and sang like an angel. But she also worked tirelessly, doing every promotional opportunity that came her way. She made fans and reporters feel like they'd been friends forever. She had a rare gift with people, because she was always true to herself with everyone she met. She trusted everyone and thought the best of most. Later, many would say that she was perhaps too trusting.

Selena was, in a word, *good*. And who was I to win her heart?

Unlike Selena, I never had anyone pushing me into music. Yet, in an odd way, it was my mother's love of music that eventually led me to Selena and the true meaning of love.

My parents were divorced by the time I was four, and my mother, my sister, and I shared a small two-bedroom apartment in San Antonio. My mother worked full-time as a payroll clerk, but we were still poor enough to need food stamps. Mom was so tired that sometimes I'd catch her crying while she washed the dishes or when she was alone in her bedroom. Sometimes she didn't eat so that my sister and I wouldn't go hungry. Still, Mom hardly complained about anything.

Music was her escape from the exhausting routines of her life, so music was always part of my life, too, like eating and breathing. We woke up every morning to her alarm clock, set to 55KTSA, a Top 40 AM radio station. In the early 1970s, disco was hot, and I loved that music as a little kid. We listened to music in the car, too, because Mom always had the radio playing when she picked us up from my grandparents' house after work.

On weekends, she'd light candles in the apartment to get it smelling good. Then she'd get on her hands and knees to clean everything. When she cleaned, the TV went off, and it was all about music. She had this really cool record collection and turned me on to classical stuff, like *The Nutcracker* and *Peter and the Wolf.* I also loved listening to story albums, where the sleeves opened like books and you could listen to the music while a narrator read the story. I never once suspected that my mother was deliberately giving me a musical education.

In middle school, I finally learned to play an instrument. My mom told me about beginner band and said that she really wanted me to try out for it, because she'd been the first chair flute player all through high school.

"Being in the school band sounds stupid," I complained.

"Trust me," she said. "Just try it."

For her, I did it. I went to the band room, where they had all of these mouthpieces set up on a table for you to try: trumpet, trombone, saxophone, clarinet, French horn, everything. I didn't know what the instruments looked like that went with those mouthpieces, or what criteria to use for choosing, but my band director let me try them all. At last I showed her the mouthpiece I liked the best, because it made this big buzzing sound when I blew on it.

"Great," the band director said. "You're going to play the French horn."

"Okay. Cool," I said.

Did I know what a French horn was? Hell, no. But she gave me this awkward black case and I had to carry it home.

So, I played the French horn—and grew to love it. I was good at it right away. I had a musical ear and I made rapid progress. I'd sit in my room and practice with the French horn and my book for hours at a time. It was really an awkward thing to have on your lap, this French horn, especially because I was a little skinny kid. It didn't help that I didn't have a music stand to prop up the book.

Eventually, I decided that I wanted to play guitar. I learned through osmosis. I had two friends who were incredible guitar players, and we all listened to the same music—Ozzy, Van Halen, Black Sabbath, Whitesnake, Mötley Crüe. I'd watch them play these songs and I'd take a snapshot with my mind so that I could remember where their hands were when they played certain chords or did these wild riffs. Then I'd go home and put my fingers in the same spots on my guitar and hit the notes.

My mom, of course, didn't want me to play electric guitar. She associated rock and roll with all of those stereotypical bad boy things, like long hair and drugs and sleeping around. It's no secret that, if you play in a band, your chances of having a girlfriend and being invited to the coolest parties are a lot higher, but I didn't do it for that. I was too busy learning new songs in my room.

For me, like Selena, music was all about being able to express myself in ways I couldn't with words. But, from the outside, I was a nobody. Or worse, I'm sure that to Abraham I was a stereotype, a ponytailed, beer-drinking hard rock guitarist in Tejano disguise. I sort of understood why he would object so strongly to me courting his daughter. He had treated her like a princess, a priceless treasure, and Selena was all that and more as a loving daughter and sister. She also embodied *his* dreams, because Abraham had always wanted to make it as a musician himself.

Maybe Selena would never have noticed me, much less fallen in love with me, if I hadn't been in her band. But I was, and that meant we were together almost twenty-four/seven some weeks. The close proximity and the fact that we were the two youngest members of the band probably played a large part in why we were drawn together at first.

But there was more to our mutual attraction than proximity. Selena knew my capacity for love even before I did, I think. She was the kind of loving daughter, sister, and friend who always told people how she felt about them, and constantly sent cards or bought little gifts for people she cared about whenever we were on the road. I had thought of myself as this tough, cool musician, but Selena told me later how impressed she was whenever she saw me playing with A.B.'s two young children.

In those early years, A.B. often brought his wife and kids with him when we toured. The children were perhaps three and six years old at the time, and they were Selena's pride and joy as an aunt. I adored them, too. Me being as relaxed a person as I am, I have always had a certain connection with kids, and I suppose when I joined the band I was still a kid myself in a lot of ways. Whenever I saw A.B.'s kids, I'd get right down on the floor and enjoy playing with them, and if Selena happened to be walking by A.B.'s hotel room and see me doing this, she'd always stop and join us.

"You're going to be a great dad someday, Chris," Selena said to me once, and I was startled by her comment, because I had never thought much about it. But it made me proud to hear her say that, too.

Selena also enjoyed meeting my friends, who are really good people, and who came around often whenever we played shows in San Antonio. I think that Selena saw how my friends were as loyal to me as I was to them, and she admired that. Selena hadn't had the same chance I had to make lifelong friendships, since she'd been on the road so much since early childhood.

Perhaps most importantly, Selena knew that I wasn't the kind of guy to object to her career, as so many men would. I wasn't jealous or possessive. I let Selena be herself, and I was willing to share her with the world—even a world where many people saw her only for who she was onstage.

I was proud of how smart Selena was, of how she brought books on the bus and earned her high school equivalency diploma, and then went on to master Spanish. I admired how much energy she put into telling kids to stay in school and stay off drugs whenever she was asked to speak at a school. She wasn't just talking the talk. She lived according to the philosophy she preached.

She had a special soft spot for fans who faced more obstacles than most. Abraham and members of the road crew would go out in the crowd and spot them, then come backstage or onto the bus and tell her all about the audience members who had struggled to come and see her. And, without fail, Selena made time for them.

"Selena!" Abraham might call, coming backstage. "There's a little girl out here in a wheelchair who really wants to meet you."

Selena would drop everything to go meet those fans and have her picture taken with them, hugging them and giving them her full-wattage smile.

She was fun, too, always dreaming up pranks. Once, we had a well-muscled security guard named Dave who made the mistake of accepting one of Selena's challenges. "I want to check out your reflexes and reaction times," she told him. "You've got to follow me and do everything I do." Selena held a Coke can in one hand; now she handed him a can of Coke, too.

"Okay, Dave," she said. "Just copy me. Let's see how fast you really are."

Selena started doing things with her Coke can, tapping it on top, putting it against her face, or stroking the can with one finger. Her motions were faster and faster as Dave followed her every move, trying to mimic her exactly.

What Dave didn't know, however, was that Selena had lined the bottom of his Coke can heavily with red lipstick, so that every time he touched his face with the bottom of the can, he marked his face. Finally we all just started laughing because we couldn't contain ourselves anymore, and Selena laughed louder than anybody else.

Onstage, of course, everyone saw a confident Selena, someone who could get the crowd eating out of the palm of her hand in minutes. She had that kind of comfort level in public. What nobody ever saw—except those of us on the bus—were her pensive moods, times when she might seem really subdued as she sat looking out the window, thinking hard about whatever was on her mind, or frowning over a new fashion design as she worked it out on paper.

I was amazed by Selena's fashion sense, and I loved looking at the sketches that she was always doing on the bus. She frequently fantasized about one day opening a clothing boutique of her own. She would always sketch her designs and then add her signature like a fancy designer's logo.

She was already starting to make her own accessories, like jeweled belt buckles, as well as designing costumes for the band. Selena would draw the designs and choose the fabric, then send everything off to a seamstress who had all of our measurements on hand.

Unfortunately, we didn't have much say in what we wore and most of the outfits didn't appeal to me. Selena's tastes were flamboyant, to say the least. She liked to see a lot of glitter and shine. I'd be handed a pair of black-and-white cowhide pants or a shiny purple satin suit with gold seams sewn down the front of the legs, and I'd say, "Oh, man. Do I really have to wear this?"

I remember an especially trying phase when Selena was all about crazy jackets that were cut short and square, with enormous shoulder pads. One particularly odious version was black on the left side and white on the right side. Meanwhile, I was listening to Nirvana and that band was wearing torn jeans and sneakers—pretty much my everyday look. Still, I loved it that Selena could create something seemingly out of thin air, visualizing ideas in her mind and then making them real through her voice and her hands.

That's the thing about Selena: she amazed me more and more every day that we spent together. This girl was getting under my skin in ways no other woman ever had. It was now to the point where I could barely stifle my feelings for her even when Abraham was around. I knew that I was in trouble even before our troubles really began.

There was kind of a ritual when the band was touring on Big Bertha. If we were far from our destination, we would all hang out in our bunks or play video games in the back lounge. The closer we got to our stop for the night, the more we all hung out in the front of the bus, looking out the windows and joking around as we eagerly anticipated being able to stretch our legs and maybe even explore a new city.

On this one particular night, everyone except Selena and I had gone to the front of the bus. She and I lingered in the bunk area, standing just a few feet apart from each other. Even with the door closed we could hear Pete clowning around to make everyone laugh.

I think that Selena and I both realized at the same time that we were alone for once. I wanted to kiss her, but I was afraid that Selena might turn me down. The strength of my feelings for her, along with this awkward situation, made me more reserved than I would have been with another woman in another place.

Nonetheless, bit by bit, we began drawing closer together as we talked. Well, to be honest, I was nervously backing up as she gradually came toward me. Selena had her back to the door leading to the front lounge area; I kept taking little steps away from her. I was breathing harder now, my face flushed and hot as I wondered, *Is this really going to happen?*

I couldn't deny my desire any longer. I was too overcome by Selena's presence, as if she were a magnet and I were merely a sliver of steel. She held me in place with her body, those eyes on mine. I stopped moving backward and leaned on the closet door with my left shoulder. Selena took another step toward me. There was nothing else that either of us could do at that moment but kiss.

And what a kiss it was. I had never kissed a woman with so much depth of feeling. There was no stopping me, or this.

We kissed for several minutes, our bodies pressed close together, despite this little voice in my head saying, *You're dead; Abraham is going to kill you.*

All of a sudden, the door to the bunk area flew open behind Selena, letting all of the noise and laughter from the front lounge spill in. Selena's face paled as we quickly broke apart. She was too frightened to turn around. Had her father seen us?

In a split second, though, I knew it was cool. The intruder wasn't Abraham, but Rick, our keyboardist and the guy I usually roomed with on the road.

"What's up, Rick?" I asked, partly to let Selena know that it was okay, and partly to downplay for Rick what he had obviously seen. I felt bad for him. He was a nice guy and freaking out, no doubt, about having seen us together, knowing how Abraham would react if he knew.

On the other hand, if I'd had to pick somebody on that bus to walk in on Selena and me kissing, I would have picked Rick. He was the least of our worries.

When we got to the hotel, Rick and I got our luggage and room keys, then walked to the corner store because it was still fairly early. Pete and Joe were rooming together as they usually did, and Selena was staying in a room with her parents and Suzette. I had just turned twenty-one a few weeks before, so it was still a novelty for me to buy alcohol; Rick and I went to the store and bought beer to bring back to the room.

Finally, safely behind the closed hotel room door, I opened a beer and tried to talk about what had happened. I decided to ask Rick straight up if he was upset with us.

"No need to worry about me," he said with a little chuckle. "But you need to be careful that Abraham doesn't find out."

For a chilly moment, I thought about what might have happened if Abraham, instead of Rick, had walked in on Selena and me. Abraham was very protective of Selena. Besides the obvious objections he might have to her seeing me—because I was in the band and I wasn't good enough for his daughter—he would also worry about her getting hurt. Abraham had seen me with other women, and he thought of Selena as young and naive. It was easy for me to imagine how he might use the threat that I wouldn't be faithful to her as ammunition.

Also, being old-school, Abraham's was the kind of marriage where his word was law, and Marcella and his children obeyed that law. He might also fear that whomever Selena married might then dictate what she did, including leave her musical career to start a family. In reality, I was the farthest you could get from being that kind of guy. I was ready to support Selena in whatever she wanted to do. But he didn't know that.

"Of course I'm going to be careful," I told Rick now. "But I can't believe what's happening."

Rick gave that little chuckle again. I could see that he, like Abraham, was thinking that I was playing Selena and trying to get something out of it, to use her in some way. But it wasn't like that and I told him so.

"This is different," I told him. "I really have feelings for Selena."

"Shut up, dude," he said at once. "Leave me out of this. The less I know, the better."

I couldn't stop talking, though. I was nervous, and this was the first time that I had talked about Selena with anybody. I kept trying to make Rick understand how serious it was, while at the same time asking questions about what might happen if Abraham found out about us.

"I don't know," Rick kept saying. "I don't know, Chris."

"Man," I said finally. "I don't know, either. Maybe I need to end this before it gets crazy. Maybe it needs to stop."

Rick just laughed. "Shut up, dude," he told me for the hundredth time. "You know you're not going to stop anything."

And I thought, *You know what, he's right. I'm not going to stop anything.* At least Rick hadn't put me down or told me to stop seeing Selena. That was almost the same thing as giving us his approval.

The hotel phone jangled on the table next to Rick's bed, startling us both. He and I stared at the phone, feeling guilty for even having this conversation. Then Rick slowly picked up the receiver and said hello.

His face broke into a grin, and then he started laughing. "Yeah, yeah. Shut up, dude. He's right here."

It was Selena. Rick always called her "dude." "Did you and Rick talk? Is he okay?" she asked anxiously.

Rick was sitting there on his bed, looking at me and shaking his head. "Yeah, we were just talking about everything," I said. "Everything is cool."

"I'm probably freaking out more than Rick is," she said with a little moan. "I can't believe how close that was. Anyway, I just wanted to call you real quick to see if you're okay."

"I'm fine," I said. "I'll see you tomorrow."

She laughed. "Not if I see you first," she said, and hung up.

"Well," I said, still looking at Rick, "I guess it's on."

Our feelings for each other began to steamroll our common sense as Selena and I continued touring with the band over the next few months. Any chance we got, we sneaked off to be alone together. Selena had no problem saying to her father, "Chris is going to the store with me for a few minutes," or, "Chris and I are going to get something to eat. We'll be right back."

Abraham would say, "Okay, you all come right back," and off we'd go.

The minute that Selena and I were out of sight, we would act like any normal couple, holding hands or walking with our arms around each other, or even chancing a breathless kiss during our precious few minutes of alone time, away from Abraham's watchful gaze.

We were always on the down low around her parents, but as the weeks turned into months, we gradually stopped caring about who else in the band knew about us. Everyone in the band had personal lives and secrets; we all had to figure ways around Abraham, who was a conservative man, a devout Jehovah's Witness, and a traditional father. We all knew how to keep secrets from him because nobody wanted to unleash his temper.

Besides, Abraham simply didn't see me as a candidate for Selena's affection, and Selena and I were so young that I'm sure most of the band members thought that our desire for each other would burn itself out and the relationship would end before long. Nobody realized the enduring bond we were forming as we fell in love—including Selena and me.

Selena usually took the lead in demonstrating our affection openly. I was too nervous about her father finding out to take much initiative. In fact, she used to love teasing me, knowing how anxious I was. I'd be hanging out in the back of the bus with Joe or Pete, or even with A.B., and she'd just come in and say, "Hey, what's going on here?" and kiss me.

That kind of display terrified Joe, because he didn't want to upset Abraham, but it was usually A.B. who would say something.

"Selena, why do you have to do that in front of us?" A.B. might ask, but Selena would crack up. Like most pesky little sisters, Selena loved getting a rise out of her big brother.

Between shows, Selena and I saw each other as much as possible. I learned more about her as time went on, yet the more time I spent with Selena, the more often she managed to surprise me. Once, for instance, we went horseback riding on the beach around the bay in Corpus, out near Mustang Island, with a few friends. The horses were calm as we rode away from the barn, and we went at a nice little pace. It all felt very romantic as the horses cruised along the shoreline while Selena and I chatted with our friends.

On the way back, though, the horses went crazy. The animals knew when they'd hit the end of the trail and could turn around; at that point, they practically wheeled in place to gallop back to the stables for feeding time or whatever.

Our friends were shouting, "Oh, shit!" as the horses raced back to the barn, terrified out of their minds. I was scared, too, but of course I was too cool to act scared in front of Selena. I was afraid that if I panicked, the horse might run even faster, too.

Meanwhile, Selena was galloping on her horse alongside mine, laughing her head off, not at all frightened. She looked as comfortable on that horse as she did onstage, and I didn't even know she could ride.

Then again, Selena wasn't like most women I knew. When I suggested fishing from the piers in Corpus, where you could rent poles, she surprised me again by being all for it. I used to fish with my Pops quite a bit—he had a little skiff, and loved to tool around in it with my mom and me—so I was comfortable baiting live fish on the hooks. Selena was thrilled when I showed her that, just by tossing a line with these small fish, you could catch a bigger fish.

Fishing in Corpus was even better than when I used to fish in the fresh water around San Antonio. In fresh water, you can have the line in the water for half an hour without getting a bite, but in salt water you'll catch something every few minutes, whether it's a keeper or not. Selena surprised me again by wanting to do everything herself. The only time I stopped her was when she caught a hardhead, a fish that's kind of like a catfish and has barblike whiskers that can really poke through your skin.

Often when I saw Selena, I would bring white roses, her favorite flower, and we were always on the phone. We also wrote love letters and cards constantly. I still have boxes of cards—she saved every card I sent her.

Selena wrote such sweet notes to me that it still hurts to read them, especially because she dated every one and I can remember what were doing on those dates. "I love looking back to where we began, seeing us as we were at the beginning," she wrote once, "then slowly leafing through the memories that we've made together to bring us to where we are today."

Eventually, everyone in the band seemed to grow more comfortable with the idea of us as a couple. It got to the point where we might be standing backstage, and she'd just come up and put her arms around me or give me a kiss in front of the whole road crew. I still hung back a little. I felt like I had to be careful, not just because of Abraham, but because I didn't want to be thought of as possessive or insecure.

Like any other relationship, ours went from one thing to the next and continued progressing. The only difference was the fast pace. Again, this was partly due to our circumstances. We weren't working nine-to-five jobs and seeing each other only on dates. We were together in the studio, at A.B.'s house, on the tour bus, and onstage. Inevitably, it was on the bus where we were finally intimate for the very first time.

We were traveling from Corpus to Dallas at the time. When we arrived at our destination and everyone began unloading things from the bus, my legs were shaking. Once again, I didn't know how to act or what to say. I remember standing outside the bus, talking to Pete, and blurting out, "I think I'm really falling in love with her," because I was that desperate to talk about it.

Pete was supportive. "Man, it's all good. Don't worry about it. I can see how she feels about you, too. Everything is going to be okay."

Just at that moment, I happened to look up at the bus and saw one of the blinds twitch in one of the side windows. My heart was pounding so hard that I could hear it in my ears, above the Dallas street traffic.

Maybe things were going to be okay. And maybe not.

That night was the first and only time I ever felt strange going up onstage with Selena. My body was still buzzing and my mind was a jumble. Everything felt upside down. Selena and I knew each other better onstage than we did in that back room of the bus; onstage, we knew each other's moves, while our private physical connection off stage was still fresh and unexplored.

We were both freaking out so much that we couldn't look at each other. Of course each of us knew where the other one was, because we had our set places and routines, but we were trying so hard to act like nothing was going on between us that we literally didn't look at each other. I kept tuning my guitar and checking the amps, when of course everything was fine.

When the show began, Selena came onstage and kept her eyes focused on the crowd. I was right behind her, on the same side as always. But, instead of looking in my direction, Selena kept looking the opposite way. We were both flustered, and then we had to kick into gear. I started playing the guitar, and she started singing, and after a few minutes things almost felt normal again.

Almost, but not quite. We both knew that something big had just happened, and that things were going to be different. After the show, I went up to her and said, "That was weird, right?"

"Yeah, that was weird," she agreed, and then she just started laughing.

"Well, for what it's worth, I'm glad that what happened, happened," I said.

She grabbed my hand quickly and then let it go, so I knew that, whatever happened from now on, we were in it together.

I never imagined that Selena and I would declare our love for each other in a Pizza Hut, but that's exactly what happened.

Whenever the band was on the road, we had a routine of meeting at the bus when it was checkout time at the hotel. The road crew would already be gone with the equipment, but we'd load our own bags onto Big Bertha and wait until everyone was there, then move on to our next destination.

Selena was almost always the last to arrive, usually because she was making last-minute clothing changes or doing her hair and makeup. It had gotten to the point where she never went out in public without looking her best; we never knew when reporters or fans or producers might be in a crowd or just waiting on the sidewalk if they saw our bus pull up.

This particular morning, though, it wasn't Selena who was last to arrive: it was Abraham. The rest of us sat talking on the bus, and Selena kept saying how hungry she was. Her favorite food was pizza with extra pepperoni; I had noticed a Pizza Hut across the street but didn't say anything about it. I assumed that Abraham was just on the phone with a promoter or something. There was no telling when he might return.

Selena, however, had spotted the Pizza Hut, too. She was going to do what she wanted—she usually did. "Want to go get pizza, Chris?" she said.

Everybody knew we had started a relationship by then, and they had our backs. The first thing Abraham would do when he returned to the bus was ask where we were, but we knew they'd just say, "She went to Pizza Hut and Chris went with her."

Abraham probably wouldn't think anything of it. In fact, he'd feel better because Selena had a chaperone. That thought made me feel bad once again about all of the sneaking around we were doing.

I thought we'd order pizza to go, but Selena wanted to sit at a table. We sat near a window so that we could see the bus. And then she just started talking, asking me about my feelings.

"I'm really happy with you," Selena said. "I love spending time with you. But I need to know where you think our relationship is headed."

I decided that I had to tell her right then how I really felt. This was a terrifying prospect. I'd had girlfriends before. I had even said I loved them, because I thought I knew what love was. But I had never experienced the feelings I had for Selena, and I told her so. I just opened up and said how happy she made me feel.

"I always look forward to seeing you and spending time with you," I said. "To be honest, I can't wait until we're going to be together again. When we're not on the road, I wish that I could speed up time so that I could be with you. And, when we're together, I wish that I could slow time down."

I told her that I didn't feel right hiding our relationship from her father. It was gnawing away at me. I was tired of the secrecy. "I wake up sometimes in the morning and feel sick, like I'm doing something wrong and just haven't been caught yet, but today's the day."

Selena nodded. She understood that, she said, but she still thought it was too soon to tell Abraham. "Let's wait for the right moment."

I wondered if there ever would be such a moment, but didn't tell her that. "Don't get me wrong," I said. "I'd never let my guilt about hiding this from your dad stop me from seeing you. It's just that, if I could change one thing, it would be that. Your dad is a great guy, and I feel like I'm betraying him. But I will always want to be with you."

I just stopped talking, then, wondering suddenly what Selena thought about everything I'd just said. I was almost holding my breath.

To my relief, Selena looked me in the eyes and said, "I love you."

That was the thing about Selena: She was one of the bravest people I've ever known, not just onstage, but in relationships. She was really quick to put her feelings out there. You always knew where you stood with her. There was no manipulation, no lying or games. Selena was purely herself, and true to who she was and what she believed in.

My heart was pounding so hard that I thought everyone in that pizza place could hear it. My pulse was racing and I just wanted to get up and shout, "Did you hear what Selena just said? She loves me!" I had never been happier in my life than I was at that moment, hearing that declaration of love from Selena.

I grinned. "I love you, too," I said.

It felt good to have taken that next step and declared our feelings aloud to each other, even as we watched out the window for Abraham. I reached across the table and took Selena's hand in mine. We just sat there for a while, touching and loving each other, secure in the knowledge that we would never let go.

Selena wore the biggest smile as we walked back to the bus. I still smile, when I remember how happy she looked that day. At the time, though, I had to scold her. "Hey, stop smiling!" I said. "You're going to give us away!"

But it wasn't Selena who put our relationship in jeopardy—it was me. A few short months after Selena and I first declared our love in that Pizza Hut, I sat in a San Antonio police station under arrest, wondering if I had destroyed the best thing in my life.

THREE

EARNING SELENA'S TRUST

C. W. Bush / Shooting Star

*I*magine how I felt as I stood in the police station, muddied and bloodied and beaten up, when the song "Ven Conmigo" started playing on the radio. It was as if Selena could see me there. At the sound of her sweet, soulful voice, my head dropped, so ashamed was I to be in this situation.

Was I going to lose the woman I loved as soon as I'd found her? Maybe I truly didn't deserve Selena. Maybe our future together was over before it had really begun.

As I waited for the police to book me, I looked back on my brief, blissful time with Selena and wondered how I could have ended up in this predicament. Everything had been going so well.

Between being on the road and working on the songs that would become our next album, *Entre a Mi Mundo*, Selena and I spent as much time as possible together during the early part of 1991. She was busier than ever with promotions, but still cheerful and energetic. That year, her duet with Alvaro Torres, "Buenos Amigos," became her first number one song. At the same time, Capitol EMI was getting ready to launch us in Mexico.

Despite her intense schedule, Selena and I had continued to see each other on the down low, escaping to restaurants, movie theaters, and anywhere else we could be alone together without word getting back to Abraham.

I had learned a lot about Selena in this time. I knew that she hated to exercise, other than an occasional jog—she definitely wasn't one of those women who would get up early and work out at the gym. She had few friends, but was close with everyone in her family—especially with her sister Suzette and her little cousin Priscilla, who was just starting middle school. She preferred magazines over books and loved to shop.

Selena and her family were Jehovah's Witnesses. They seldom talked about their faith with me—or with anyone else, for that matter. I had been raised Catholic and had let my faith lapse; I didn't know much about Jehovah's Witnesses and thought it must be some kind of radical religion. Sometimes, though, Selena and her family would talk about religion on the bus, and I realized that they used the same Bible I'd grown up with and understood its teachings much better than I did. They lived according to their deeply held values. This made me start thinking about God and the point of faith in our lives in ways that I never had before.

What struck me about Selena more than anything else during this time, though, was her compassion. Her compassion encompassed her friends, her family, her fans—especially those who were struggling in their lives with illness or poverty—women in crisis, children, and even animals.

I remember one time when we were driving alone together and Selena hit a dove. She wasn't speeding or anything; Selena and I were just jamming to the radio cranked up loud when a flock of doves shot up from the side of the road and started to fly.

This one little dove was slower than the others. It started flying straight along the road ahead of us, and we came up on that poor bird so fast that we hit it. The windshield popped him right on his tail feathers and then the dove flew off. I swear that for a second I could see that bird's surprised face as he curved off.

The bird wasn't hurt, but Selena had to pull the car over to the side of the road, she was crying so hard. She was almost hysterical. "I hit that little bird!" she said, sobbing. "I killed it!"

"No, you didn't," I reassured her. I leaned over to hug her, holding her close while she cried. "I saw the bird fly off. It's going to be fine. You didn't even hit it that hard."

Selena sat up again and dried her eyes. "Really? You think the bird is okay?"

"I do," I said.

At the same time, we both noticed this little streak on the windshield. I knew it couldn't have been from the bird, but Selena made me clean the windshield before she started driving again. "I just can't stand to hurt anything," she explained.

Because I was in the band, Abraham had continued to allow Selena to spend time with me without questioning either of us about it. I'm sure he thought that, at least if Selena was with me, she was still beneath the protective umbrella of her family.

Meanwhile, I was growing ever more uncomfortable with the idea that I was betraying this man who had trusted me. I cared about Abraham on a personal level, yet ever since that fateful trip to Mexico, Selena and I had been dishonest. Now I had been arrested and could very well serve jail time, proving to Abraham that I wasn't worthy of Selena—even before he knew our relationship had begun!

Standing in that police station in San Antonio, I wondered if my thoughtless, stupid actions of this one night were going to cost me the trust of the one woman who had ever managed to break through my defenses and show me what real love felt like—and destroy any hope I might have had of winning her father's approval.

The evening had started out well enough. I was at a bar in San Antonio with my cousin and a friend when another friend called and asked if we wanted to meet him somewhere else.

"Sure," I said, forgetting that I'd already been drinking and probably shouldn't be going anywhere.

We headed out on the highway in my mom's Oldsmobile. I was driving about eighty miles an hour—over the speed limit, of course, but in Texas the highways are straight and wide, and that night there was little traffic. We were cruising along, talking and listening to music, when I happened to glance in the rearview mirror and see a police car with its lights on. The cop car was so far behind me that it never occurred to me that I might be the one in his sights.

When I took the exit off highway 90 heading west, the cop came off the ramp behind me. He was coming at me really fast. And then, all of a sudden, there were two police cars coming straight at me, head on. They wheeled around and parked across the road in front of my car to form a barricade. Then the doors swung open and the cops were out of the cars, aiming shotguns at us.

I jammed on the brakes and pulled over to the side of the road. My friend in the backseat just sat there, terrified. My cousin, who was in the front seat next to me, started yelling and swearing. One of the cops came up to the car, yanked open the door and grabbed him by the hair. The cop pulled him out of the car while another officer helped him throw my cousin down on the ground.

I lost it when I saw that. There were six police officers and just the two of us. They had guns, and we were unarmed. My friend remained where he was, afraid to do anything, but I went ballistic. My cousin had protected me through a lot of things as a kid, and this was patently unfair.

There was a brawl by the side of the road, and of course we lost. Within minutes my cousin and I were in handcuffs and being led to the police cars. They let my friend go.

"Run, don't walk," one of the cops advised him. "Do not even turn around."

My friend took off down the highway. In the police car, I tried to calm down my cousin, who was swearing and kicking the seat.

They took us to the police station and booked us. Our clothes were torn, and we were muddy and bruised. Things looked bad for us all around. The police had reported that their car had been right behind us with its lights on, and that they'd seen me turn around, see the lights, then gun the car and initiate a high-speed chase. None of that was true, but I could see that it was going to be very difficult to defend myself. It was going to be my word against theirs.

So here I was, standing in line with the other criminals in a big room waiting to get my mug shot and fingerprints done. All I could think about was Selena, who worked so hard to convey the kind of image that would get her family ahead in the music business— respectable, clean, kind, and professional at all times—while I'd done something that could potentially stain the Quintanilla family's stellar reputation.

Thank God nobody knows about us, I thought. Selena was really starting to get a lot of airtime, especially in Texas, and she had won several Tejano music awards. Plus, she had a "good girl" image to uphold for her Coca-Cola sponsorship. If people linked us together, things really could blow up in a bad way for her and the band.

As I stood there hanging my head and hearing Selena's mournful, powerful voice fill the air, one of the station guards recognized me—possibly because he was aware of the song on the radio, too. I also stood out in a crowd because not many people wore their hair in a ponytail the way I did, with the sides of my head shaved short.

The guard took me aside and asked, "What happened? What are you doing here?"

When I told him, he helped me make a phone call and get out of processing fast, then told me where the car was impounded.

All I could think about as I left the police station that night was talking to Selena. I called her right away, knowing that she had probably been trying to reach me and was worrying when I was nowhere to be found.

To my relief, Selena reacted calmly. She came down hard on me for drinking and driving, and rightfully so, but she also saw my side of things and thought the police had overreacted.

I decided to wait and tell Abraham in person. As I boarded the bus for our next tour, I said, "Hey, Abraham. I have to talk to you. I got into a situation the other day, and I want you to hear it from me, not from anyone else."

I was a hundred percent straight with him and told Abraham everything, despite the fact that my head was buzzing because I was so scared. The upshot of the incident was that I was going to have a court date, and then I'd probably be on probation and have to do community service.

Abraham didn't go off the way I was afraid he would. Instead, he just nodded and said, "Chris, I'm sure everything's going to be okay.

But you've got to be careful. We don't want you getting hurt. Besides, the band has a lot of good things coming up, and you don't want to miss that." Then he actually gave me a hug.

Abraham gave great hugs. He opened his arms wide, and you had no choice but to walk right into them. The hug, of course, made me feel worse than ever. I was extremely happy to be forgiven—while at the same time feeling terrible that I was still keeping my relationship with Selena a secret from him.

Selena and I were still seeing each other any chance we got. This meant that I spent a lot of time in Corpus, so that Selena never had to lie—other than by omission. She would announce that she was going out to run some errands, then swing by to pick me up at a hotel and I'd run the errands with her. We went out in her car, which even now makes me shudder, because it would have been so easy to run into someone she knew. Corpus Christi isn't that big a place, and Selena's reputation as a singer was spreading fast.

"I don't even care if somebody sees us," Selena would say, taking my hand or putting her arms around me even in public, while I was always warily watching over one shoulder.

Then, one morning, she realized just how much of a risk we were taking. I was staying in one of the hotels on the opposite side of the harbor bridge from downtown Corpus, where I always felt like we were safer, because a big body of water lay between the Quintanilla family and me. Selena drove over to meet me, as she usually did.

When we were ready to leave the hotel room, Selena went out first, acting as cool and at ease about the whole situation as ever. She was the sort of person who always loved taking risks. I spent a few extra minutes packing my shoulder bag, tucking away my sunglasses, wallet, and checkbook.

Suddenly Selena bolted back into the room and slammed the door behind her. "Oh no!" she cried. "I forgot that my aunt works here. I think she just saw me coming out of the room!"

"What aunt?" I asked, panicked.

"She's married to my dad's brother. It's really bad if she saw us."

I had to laugh. "Look at you," I teased. "Miss 'I don't care, I'm so cool.'"

"Shut up!" Selena snapped. "Seriously, Chris. If my aunt sees us, it's going to be crazy."

We waited a while, then sneaked out of that hotel *Mission: Impossible* style. "Guess I'd better cross this place off my list," I said, once we were safely on the road.

Sometimes Selena and I saw each other when I came to Corpus to work on songs with A.B., too. I really enjoyed working with Selena's brother. He and I had a few run-ins now and then, but he always gave me a lot of freedom as a guitarist and really encouraged me to develop my own musical style. Maybe we hit it off because he was a talker and I was a listener, and he always had a strong opinion whereas I was pretty easygoing. Who knows? In any case, we developed a strong friendship.

Like me, A.B. had once wanted to be a rock musician, not Tejano. His rock career had come to a screeching halt because Abraham had insisted on forming a family band to play Tejano music. A.B. had no choice but to play songs other people had written that he didn't like. Finally, he began to write his own songs and record them—eventually winning awards for his songwriting.

Selena found every way she could to tease A.B., especially when he and I were trying to work on some music. She'd come over to A.B.'s house, put her arms around me from behind while I was playing guitar, and give me a hug and a kiss.

"Come on, guys," A.B. would say. "Right in front of me? Really?"

Not long after my run-in with the San Antonio police, I got into another scrape that probably caused the Quintanilla family to wonder what Selena ever saw in me—and made Selena herself almost call it quits because she was so fed up.

We were working on songs that would become our new album, *Entre a Mi Mundo*, at a studio in San Antonio, and the band was staying at a local hotel. Since I lived in the city I didn't stay there, but after the recording session I went to the hotel with the band to celebrate. Late in the evening, I found myself in one of the hotel rooms with two brothers who were members of the road crew and we started drinking heavily.

At one point, the brothers started wrestling, and before long it became a free-for-all among the three of us. It got really crazy in there; for instance, we weren't trying to break the door on purpose, but one of us got thrown into it and knocked the door right off its hinges. There were a couple of holes in the wall, too, where one of the brothers threw me over his back and my feet hit the wall.

Being buzzed like that means that you don't notice what's happening at the time. I was just pumped up. A friend of mine came by, and I eventually left the hotel with him and went back to my apartment.

Joe, our keyboard player, had been out in San Antonio having a good time somewhere else. He told me later that he came back to that room and plopped down on the bed. When he felt glass on the bedspread, he said, "What the hell?" But by then the two brothers were passed out on the other bed, so he just brushed off the glass and went to sleep. He woke up with a woman standing over him, going down a checklist on a clipboard.

Joe sat up, looked around the room, said, "Oh, shit," and bailed. He hid in one of the other hotel rooms, knowing what Abraham's response would be to the room being trashed.

I knew nothing about any of this until later that morning, when Selena came to my apartment. I stumbled over to the door, still half asleep, and opened it when I heard her knocking and shouting my name.

Selena wouldn't even cross the threshold into my apartment. She was so furious that she just stood right there in the doorway and let me have it. The two members of the road crew had already been fired, she told me. She didn't know what Abraham and A.B. would do about me. But she didn't care.

"That's it!" Selena shouted. "We're over! I don't want to be with anybody like this. I can't believe you! How could you let yourself drink so much and let things get out of control like that?"

There was nothing I could say in my defense. I just listened and watched the woman I loved walk out of my life because I knew that I had done the wrong thing. What the hell was I thinking? Selena was right. I didn't deserve to be with her.

I waited anxiously for Abraham or A.B. to call. I fully expected to be fired and I was miserable, not just because my stupidity had caused Selena to leave me, but because we were finishing up an album that Abraham was sure would launch our careers in Mexico and the rest of Latin America. Selena y Los Dinos would move on and leave me behind.

As more time went by without any phone calls, I grew increasingly agitated. What had happened? Did the other two guys take the heat for me, and not mention me being there? Much as I would have liked to escape Abraham's wrath, that wouldn't be right, I decided. I knew that I had to tell the truth, apologize, and try to make amends. That was the very least I could do for the Quintanilla family.

Finally I drove to the studio, where I knew I'd find Abraham. He was in the control room with one of our sound engineers, watching Selena record a vocal track. She saw me come in but ignored me.

I joined Abraham, not knowing whether I was going to be fired on the spot, or if he'd ask me to finish the record first, then go. I told him what had happened at the hotel the night before, holding nothing back.

"I'm sorry," I said. "Nothing like that will ever happen again. I let things get out of hand. I didn't stop it. I don't know what else to tell you, but I apologize, and I will pay for all of the damages."

To my shock, Abraham accepted my apology. He knew that I meant what I said. He even put his arm around me and, once again, reassured me. "Everything will be all right, Chris."

My face burned with shame. Why had the other two men been fired, while Abraham was willing to give me a second chance? I like to think that, even then, he saw me as a son. In any case, once again, I was nearly crippled with guilt by my deception. I was being honest with this man I respected—but not completely.

On the other hand, things were over with Selena and me. What did it matter now? For just an instant, I even let myself think that maybe it was in Selena's best interest to break things off with me.

Abraham told me that he had an errand to run. "You going to be here for a while?"

I thought of Selena in the studio, and nodded. "Just a bit," I said.

"Good. Keep an eye on her," Abraham said, and took off.

"Okay."

Selena finished singing and came into the control room. I had been standing behind the engineer. Now she stood right next to me, her arm rubbing against mine, and said, "What's going on?"

"Nothing," I said, my arm tingling. "I came to apologize to your dad. I told him everything."

"What's the deal?" she asked.

"We're cool."

"You're going to keep playing with us?"

"Yes."

Immediately, she put her arms around me and pressed her body close.

"Wait a minute," I asked, laughing. "I thought you just broke up with me and we weren't together anymore."

"Shut up," she said.

"No." I turned to her. "In all seriousness, I need to apologize to you, too." I told her my plan to pay for all of the damages, and added, "I hope I didn't embarrass you too much. You know that I'd never deliberately do anything to hurt you. I don't want to lose you."

She hugged me hard. "Of course you're not going to lose me. I'm right here."

We stayed like that for a long time, despite the fact that the engineer was in the control room with us, having to act like he didn't see or hear anything at all.

By this time, I had started telling just a few close friends about Selena. I had also told my parents that we were seeing each other. I knew they would be supportive, but the first time I brought Selena home to meet my mother and stepfather, she was extremely nervous.

Selena was about to perform in San Antonio, so she was dressed for the stage in a glamorous red outfit and she'd brushed her shoulder-length hair out. "I want to look my best when I meet your mom," she confided shyly.

The meeting between Selena and my mother went well, I told her later. I could tell that my mom liked her.

Still, Selena said, "I was more nervous about meeting your mom than I was about going onstage tonight."

After that night, however, Selena spent a lot of time at my mother's house whenever she came to San Antonio. She had an excuse to do that now, because she had found shops in San Antonio that sold leather, jewelry, beads, and other things that she needed to make her belts and costumes. Looking back at pictures of her during that time, you can see her wearing these big rhinestone belt buckles that she used to make.

Selena would tell her family that she was shopping in San Antonio, and then she would come see a movie with me, or we'd go out to eat. We weren't as afraid of being recognized in the city, though I was still on guard. Selena would want to walk with her arm around me, but I'd say, "Hey, you know how much I want to be affectionate with you in public and all that, but until you think your dad's ready to hear about us, we've got to be careful."

Sometimes, Selena would just come hang out at my mom's house. She was more relaxed with my mother than she was with almost anyone else, probably because she was away from all of the things pulling at her—and because my mom accepted us as a couple. Selena used to sit in the glider in the backyard, just swinging and talking to my mother. She also loved taking walks with my mom around the neighborhood because it was quiet and nobody ever recognized her.

She enjoyed watching my stepfather cook, too. Once, he had bought a big roast with a bone. While we were in the kitchen talking, Selena watched Pops, mesmerized, as he cut up the meat for stew and set the bone aside. She was fascinated by these small domestic details because she had been on the road for so many years with her family.

"What are you going to do with that bone?" she asked.

"I'm going to make soup," Pops said.

"Really? You can use a bone to make soup?" She was amazed.

Another night, when my mom suggested a walk, Selena asked if she could walk to the corner barefooted.

Startled, my mother told her that of course she could. "But why do you want to?"

"I just want to feel the warm cement on the soles of my feet," Selena said. "I never get to do that."

Another afternoon, I was outside washing the car with my stepfather. Selena and my mom had just come back from shopping when all of a sudden the ice cream truck came by. Selena ran back outside, all excited. "Can we get some ice cream, Chris? Can we go to the truck?"

I laughed and said sure. Selena made a beeline for that truck, reminding me again of all of the simple things about childhood that I'd taken for granted that Selena never had. She had given up her childhood to make music and go on the road with her family.

She never complained about it, but Selena was never really allowed to be a carefree child the way most of us are. Sometimes I felt that loss for her. I was happy to give her at least a glimpse into the way ordinary people lived. Looking back, I only wish that I could have given her more.

FOUR

FACING A FATHER'S WRATH

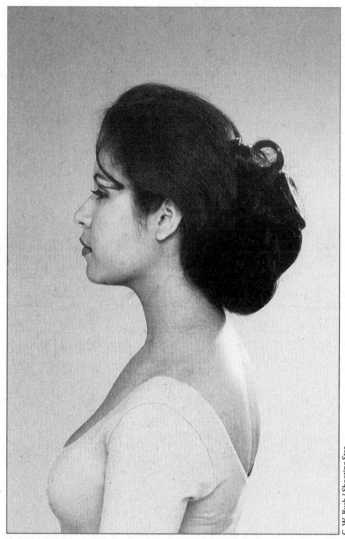

*U*ltimately, it wasn't anything that Selena and I did that brought our relationship to Abraham's attention and brought his wrath down upon us both. It was her sister, Suzette.

We had just finished playing a show in El Campo, Texas. Selena and I were hanging out on Big Bertha while the road crew broke down the equipment. Everyone else was either outside or in the bar as she and I relaxed in the front lounge area of the bus. We weren't doing anything suspicious. We weren't even sitting next to each other; I was seated at the table and Selena sat on the couch across from me. We had changed our clothes and were just talking when we heard the bus door swing open.

Instinctively, Selena and I both straightened up and fell silent as someone ascended the steps of the bus. It was only Suzette. Before I had time to feel relieved and make a joke, however, I saw from Suzette's expression that she wasn't as pleased to see us as we were to see her.

"Oh, God," Suzette said. She rolled her eyes at us, then spun around and got off the bus again, slamming the door so hard that the bus rocked a little.

Selena and I exchanged puzzled glances. "What was that all about?" I asked.

"No idea," Selena said.

It never occurred to either of us that Suzette would go to her father at that moment and tell him about us. Why would she? Suzette and I had always been friends. Like the rest of the band, she knew about Selena and me; she had already told us, "Look, I'm not involved in what you're doing together. And if Dad asks me, I'm going to say that I don't know anything."

A few minutes later, the door to the bus swung open again. This time it was Abraham. He climbed the steps but stopped near the driver's seat, staring straight at me.

"Chris, can you come here for a second?" he asked. He appeared calm, but his mouth was set and his voice was hoarse from either fatigue or tension.

"Sure." I got up from the table, alarm bells sounding in my head.

"What's going on?" Selena asked.

I shrugged and followed her father. By the time I reached the top of the bus steps, Abraham was standing on the ground again, just waiting. His dark eyes were hard and his shoulders were pulled back. What was going on?

We had performed in Houston the night before; Abraham had been paid for that show in cash and had somehow rushed out of the hotel room in the morning without retrieving his briefcase full of money from under the bed. By the time he remembered, we were already setting up for the show in El Campo. Abraham decided to borrow a car from my friend Carlos, whose band was opening for us that night, so that he could race back to Houston, feverishly hoping that by some stroke of luck the money would still be there.

It was, thankfully. Still, I reminded myself that this mishap had caused Abraham to miss our show in El Campo—and had probably made him even more exhausted and irritable than he usually was, particularly since he had nobody to blame for that mistake but himself.

As I joined him on the street, I ticked off every other possible reason that Abraham might feel compelled to call me aside like this, too. None of the reasons seemed like good ones. Had I said or done something to set him off?

Abraham was certainly angry. He started to walk away, his shoulders hunched forward and his hands balled into fists. Thinking, *Oh, man, please don't let him try to do anything*, I followed him toward the back of the bus, where the generator was making a loud clacking sound.

Suddenly Abraham stopped so fast that I nearly ran into him. He wheeled around and pointed a finger at me. "Suzette just told me that she walked onto the bus and saw you and Selena holding hands," he said. "I don't know what's going on with you guys, but whatever it is, it stops right now."

I remained silent as Abraham continued to yell and jab his finger in my direction, trying to intimidate me. "And one more thing!" he finished. "If you say a single word about this conversation to Selena, I will deny it and she's going to believe me."

What had made Suzette say something to him? To this day, I have no idea. It was probably just a rift between sisters—nothing serious, just a bad mood.

I could have denied holding hands with Selena. That was the truth, after all. But I didn't bother. Abraham had good reason to be accusing me. Besides, I was tired of living with the worry that, every day, Selena and I were doing something wrong by loving each other and hiding it from her father.

I had known that, sooner or later, Abraham would discover our secret, and this worry had been a constant thorn in my side. Here we were, so happy and so in love, yet there was this one thing that I constantly itched to fix. More than for me, I wanted to fix the situation for Selena's sake. She worked harder and was more generous than anyone I'd ever met. She deserved to have her father's blessing and have people be happy for her.

I didn't want to lie to Abraham anymore. At the same time, I also didn't want to defy him or make him any angrier than he already was. If there were any right words or right deeds I could have done to change his mind about Selena and me, I would have done them. I just didn't know what they were.

So I just said, "Okay." What else was there to say? All I wanted at the moment was to defuse the situation. My only other option would have been to tell him, "No, I'm not going to stop seeing Selena." I had a pretty good idea how that would go over.

Thankfully, my response seemed to satisfy him. Abraham turned on his heel and stormed off. He must have thought he'd won. He didn't know how serious my relationship with Selena already was. He certainly didn't suspect that Selena and I were already lovers, or that we saw each other nearly every day when we weren't touring. In his view, his daughter and I were just two kids who'd started flirting. In love? Impossible.

Once Abraham had huffed back into the building with the road crew, I rejoined Selena on the bus. "I think your sister told your father that she came on the bus and saw us holding hands," I said.

Selena was furious; she wanted to go after Suzette and have it out with her. I had to calm her down. I didn't want Selena arguing with Suzette in front of everyone. What good would that do? Everyone we cared about except Abraham had already been told about us, or had seen us express our feelings for each other in some way—my mom, Selena's mom, my friend Carlos and his mom, our friends, everyone in the band—so fighting out in the open could only make things worse with Abraham.

Things were incredibly tense on the bus in the days after that. I was trying to walk a fine line between keeping Selena happy and making everyone else happy, too, including her father and the band. I didn't want to lose my job. And, stupidly, I kept thinking that once Abraham calmed down, we would all be able to talk openly about what was going on and he'd accept the situation.

That didn't happen. Instead, Abraham grew increasingly difficult to be around. He was in danger of losing his little girl—and his star—and his guard was up. The band members, including A.B. and Suzette, turned their backs on me, scarcely speaking to me unless it was absolutely essential to the work we were doing.

Meanwhile, I continued to act like nothing was going on between Selena and me. I didn't want to act disrespectfully in front of Abraham, nor did I want to jeopardize my position in the band. I loved playing with Los Dinos. I also knew how upset Selena would be if I weren't able to play with them.

I was frankly surprised that Abraham let me stay. He must have assumed that I was going to do whatever he said. Everyone else did. Besides, how could I possibly be a threat, or worthy of his daughter's affection? He was in charge of his family and his band. I was just a lowly guitarist, and musicians were a dime a dozen.

At the same time, Abraham was now on high alert for any potential trouble within the ranks. He kept a sharp eye on us and made sure that, ninety-nine percent of the time, he was with Selena everywhere she went. Little did he know that Selena and I were still seeing each other in San Antonio and Corpus whenever the band wasn't on the road.

Naturally, it hurt my feelings when the other band members shunned me. I thought we were friends, but now they made it clear that nobody had my back. On the other hand, what did I expect? Like me, nobody wanted to lose his job or mess with Abraham. They weren't telling me not to see Selena, so I guess that was their way of showing some support for us, but that was about as far as it went.

At one point, A.B. and I were sitting together on the bus when we happened to notice Abraham pacing slowly back and forth on the sidewalk below, clearly moping. I wanted to go down there and tell Abraham how I felt about Selena, but I knew there was nothing I could say that wouldn't provoke another fit of rage.

"Dude, I hate this," I told A.B.

"Hate what?" he asked.

"I hate it that it's so hard for your dad to think about Selena and me being together."

"Don't worry," A.B. reassured me. "Dad will get over this. You've just got to give him some time."

Man, I said to myself. *I don't see that ever happening.*

Despite all of this exhausting tension, Selena and I were still happy together. We always had a great time going out to eat, hanging at my mom's house in San Antonio, or visiting friends who knew about and accepted our relationship.

One of my favorite memories is of a time I visited Selena in Corpus Christi and we ended up taking a long walk by the water. We walked all the way to the tip of one of the jetties, where we sat and talked about our situation, promising each other once again that nothing could ever tear us apart.

As we sat there, Selena put her head on my shoulder and started softly singing one of my favorite songs, "More than Words," by a phenomenal band called Extreme that I'd introduced to her not long before. Those lyrics seemed to describe our feelings for one another perfectly.

I had never been more content than I was at that moment, sitting on that jetty in Corpus and having Selena sing to me. How amazing it was, I thought, that this woman I loved so much would sing for me, and me alone, in her incredible voice, as the water sparkled silver beneath a wide blue Texas sky.

After Selena passed away, Extreme came to Corpus to play. The band dedicated that song to her because I had met them once and told the lead singer how much Selena loved the lyrics. But that was later, after everything.

The day that Abraham finally threw me out of Los Dinos started out like any other day. We were again traveling on the bus. We had just finished a show and we were all sitting up toward the front. The atmosphere still crackled with tension. The band members were clearly getting tired of this whole situation and mostly ignoring me. I'm sure they wished I'd leave so that peace could reign in their world once again.

No single discussion or event sparked Abraham's anger, but his blood was boiling. Looking back on that day, I'm guessing that he had been obsessing over the possibility that Selena and I were still sneaking around, and he just couldn't take it anymore.

For whatever reason, as we were driving home from the show, Abraham hit the brakes, pulled the bus over to the side of the road, turned around, and started yelling at me from the driver's seat. "That's it! This is over between you and Selena! It stops now. This is not going to happen!"

I glanced out of the window, quickly weighing my options. We had been in a small town just a few miles back; Abraham had at least pulled the bus off the road. I could walk back to that town and call a friend to pick me up if things on the bus got too intolerable.

Still shouting, Abraham was now walking toward me, yelling at both Selena and me about how we'd tried to play him for a fool. "This thing between you and Chris, whatever it is, it's not going to happen!" he shouted at Selena. "He has nothing to offer you!"

Selena started arguing with him. Meanwhile, I felt caught. I knew that if I reacted the way I really wanted to, by jumping in and shouting to express my own anger at the insults Abraham was hurling in my direction, things could only get worse.

I suddenly felt exhausted, thinking, *Really? This has to happen? Why?*

It must have looked like I was just passively sitting there, taking everything Abraham threw my way. Finally I got out of my seat and stood next to Selena to show my support.

Abraham glared at me. "You know what you are? You're like a cancer in my family!"

"Don't talk to him that way!" Selena yelled. "I love Chris and he loves me!"

"Of course he loves you!" Abraham shouted back. "You're beautiful and you're rich!"

They went back and forth while I stood there. I was more hurt than angry that Abraham would say those things. I understood why he was afraid of losing Selena, but he'd known me long enough to know I wasn't the kind of guy who would be motivated by money.

"If this foolishness continues between you two, I'm going to end this band!" Abraham declared when Selena wouldn't back down.

I glanced around the bus. I knew that Abraham would never end the band. It meant too much to him. But I saw that everybody else looked pretty freaked out. I felt more exhausted than ever. I just wanted out. I was tired of having these nervous feelings, like I was doing something wrong by falling in love with Selena. I was sick of being around Abraham, who was doing everything possible to make my life miserable.

In the middle of the argument, just like that, I said, "I'm out of here. Screw this. I'll find my own way home. I don't want to ride in here anyway."

"You can't leave!" Selena cried.

I gave her a quick embrace. "He's your dad, Selena," I whispered. "I love you, but this is too much stress for me. I have my family. This is yours."

She knew I was right. There was nothing else that could happen. Certainly Abraham and I weren't going to be able to smooth things out by talking. He was too angry and upset for that to happen.

I got off, took a few deep breaths of cool night air, and started walking along the highway as the bus pulled back onto the road with a roar of exhaust.

I had left one of my guitars on the bus when I walked off that night. A few days later, I asked Jesse, a good friend of mine, to get the guitar for me when Selena y Los Dinos played in San Antonio.

Afterward, Jesse told me what happened. As he had searched out the road crew and asked for my guitar, Abraham approached him. Abraham knew that Jesse and Selena were friends, because he had heard a message from Jesse recently on Selena's phone.

"What do you want to talk to Selena about?" Abraham demanded.

"Girlfriend problems," Jesse said. This was the truth.

"What about your friend Chris?" Abraham asked. "Is he still seeing Selena?"

"I don't know," Jesse said.

"Come on," Abraham said. "You're best friends, right? I know Chris tells you everything. Don't try to bullshit me."

"What do you have against them being together?" Jesse asked.

Abraham laughed. "Chris has nothing to offer. He's got no money and no future. He's just a bum musician."

"He's my friend," Jesse said. "I don't want to hear you talk that way. And he and Selena love each other."

"Chris and Selena aren't going to be together!" Abraham shouted, as Jesse turned away to leave.

Because I was no longer with Los Dinos, Abraham had no way of keeping tabs on me. Selena told me that the band members, though supportive of us as a couple, were frankly relieved that I was off the bus. A.B. had hired back their old guitarist and that was that, or so everyone thought.

I knew that Selena and I were going to stay together. I wasn't thinking about marriage at that point—Selena and I were still kids—but I definitely knew that I was in love and wanted to be with her.

Back in San Antonio, I continued living in my father's apartment and playing music. I felt free now to tell everyone about my relationship with Selena and what had happened with her family. It was odd, in a way, to find myself surrounded by people who loved me. I had been immersed in Selena's family and in Los Dinos for so long that I'd forgotten what it felt like to have so much support. I was reminded of how good my friends and family are.

I started playing music with my friends Rudy and Albert. We managed to land some gigs, and I made decent money. All in all, I was doing fine. More than fine: for me, the pressure was off. I talked to Selena regularly on the phone and we saw each other whenever and however we could. She was still on the road a lot, but that was okay; I was busy working on the weekends and she was, too. We still had our weekdays together.

Freed of that nerve-racking situation with her father and the other members of Los Dinos, I started to enjoy my life again. Selena, though, was still suffering, having to live with the guilt of sneaking around with me behind her father's back. She was filled with that same nervous energy I'd been feeling before I got out of the band.

Selena had always been a risk taker, but that energy compelled her to do some even crazier things while we were apart. One night, for instance, Selena called to say that she'd hurt herself bungee jumping.

"You did what?" I frowned at the phone receiver, sure I'd heard her wrong.

I hadn't. Selena had been at a carnival with friends. One of the attractions was a tall platform where you could climb up a ladder, put on a harness attached to a bungee cord, and jump off. Selena had twisted her back in the fall; she even went to see a chiropractor, yet the pain was still acute.

"What the heck were you thinking, doing something that dangerous?" I asked. "What was going through your head to make you want to do that?"

"They dared me," she said.

I had to laugh. As I'd discovered with Selena, it was a mistake to dare her to do anything, because ninety-nine point nine percent of the time, she would take the dare.

"So how did it feel to do it?" I asked.

"It was pretty scary jumping off and going toward the ground," she said. "But the really scary part was, just when I was breathing a sigh of relief, the cord pulled me back up and I knew I'd have to come down again. The second time was definitely worse than the first. I will never do that again!"

About a month after leaving Los Dinos, I spent the day in San Antonio with Selena. We went out to eat, did some shopping, and then hung out at my mom's house. In just the short time I had been with her, I could feel myself opening up, becoming more loving and generous with everyone I knew. I always told my mom and dad that I loved them now, just as Selena did with the people she cared about. I even bought small gifts for people on impulse, because I'd seen how happy those gifts made Selena feel when she bought them—and I'd experienced the joy my friends felt when I remembered them. I never in a million years would have become a generous person if it hadn't been for Selena showing me the way.

That particular day, Selena had escaped to see me in San Antonio by explaining to her family that she needed to run some errands and would eat dinner with some girlfriends. I had to push her to leave my mother's house, finally, because I didn't want her driving late at night and getting questioned at home.

"Let me take you back to your apartment, at least," Selena said, wrapping her arms around my waist.

"No, no. I'll call Jesse to come get me," I said. "It's already getting late. Plus I want to be on the phone with you when you're driving back."

Selena and I could talk for hours; within a few minutes of Selena leaving, we were deep into our phone conversation. Suddenly, my mother's doorbell rang. It was after dark. Nobody ever came to my mother's house this late. *Who could it be?* I wondered.

I was still on the phone with Selena. "Hang on," I said and walked over to the window to peer through the blinds.

Abraham's car was parked out front. I panicked. How had he tracked me down here? Then I remembered that I'd put my mother's address on the payroll forms when I joined the band.

"Oh my God," I said to Selena. "Your dad is outside."

"What?" she shrieked. "What's he doing there?"

"I don't know. I'm going to hang up and find out. I'll call you back," I promised, and started down the hall, the phone still in my hand.

Clearly, Abraham was here to confront me. Maybe he was even checking to see if Selena was here.

Before I could make it down the hall to the front door, my step-father opened it. I came around the corner of the hall and saw Pops with the front door slightly open. He had poked his head outside a little.

"Can I help you, sir?" Pops asked in a stern voice.

That's when I saw that Pops had a gun in his hand. The pistol was older than I was and I'd never seen him use it; he kept that gun around only to scare intruders.

Pops had met Abraham before and knew who he was. He knew what Abraham was doing to Selena and me, too, and he didn't like it. I guess this was his way of showing his displeasure.

"Hey, Abraham, what's going on?" I called from behind my step-father.

Pops turned around and said, "Oh, you know this man?"

"Yeah, Pops," I said, keeping one eye on the gun. "That's Abra-ham, Selena's dad."

My stepfather opened the door a little bit wider and moved out of the way. Still, he kept looking Abraham up and down, his face saying, *Just try something. Go ahead.*

I didn't like it that my stepfather was carrying a gun. At the same time, I thought it was great that Abraham—a man so used to in-timidating others, a man accustomed to having the whole world revolve around him—was seeing that I had friends and family, too.

I didn't invite Abraham inside. I walked down the front walk toward his car, knowing he'd have to follow me, and said, "What's up, Abraham?"

"Have you spoken to Selena?" he said.

His voice was surprisingly friendly, but maybe that had some-thing to do with the gun. "No," I said. "Why?"

I felt terrible for lying. At the same time, I didn't want to make things harder on Selena than they already were. I wasn't about to tell Abraham that I'd spent the whole day with his daughter and that he'd missed her by just a few minutes.

"She's supposed to be home, that's all," Abraham said. "I was worried."

"I'm sure she'll be home soon," I said. "You would have heard if something had happened."

We had reached Abraham's car, and that's when I saw the map folded on the front seat in that awkward way maps get folded when people are in a hurry. This guy really had hunted me down. He wasn't about to give up trying to destroy whatever was between Selena and me. He just had no idea that our love would be such a formidable opponent.

FIVE

A SECRET WEDDING

Courtesy of the author

$\mathcal{S}$elena and I were in a holding pattern for the next couple of months. Her father continued to see me as a threat, she said. Abraham was worried that if Selena was with me, I might pull her out of the band, and all of the work he'd done would "go down the tubes," as he put it to Selena. He showed no signs of relenting no matter how much Selena argued, begged, or cried.

Then, on April 2, 1992, I woke up in a Corpus Christi hotel room to the sound of someone pounding on the door.

I had seen Selena the night before and spent the night in Corpus because we were out until late. My hotel, the Gulf Beach II on Surfside Boulevard, was on the other side of the harbor bridge from the city, and I usually stayed here whenever I visited Selena. We felt safer and more secluded if we were on the other side of the bridge from her family.

In fact, nobody we hung out with in Corpus ever crossed the bridge much, so I didn't have to worry about somebody seeing my car and word getting back to Abraham that I was in town. I had the feeling that he probably drove around to every hotel in Corpus Christi, Texas, looking for Selena and me whenever she wasn't home at sunset. For that reason, she never spent the night with me.

Selena had been valiantly keeping up her performance schedule despite her disagreements with her father—she was a professional, and she knew that her family's livelihood, as well as her reputation, depended on her showing up to do the gigs Abraham booked for the band. I knew that Selena was due to leave early that morning for a show in El Paso. I didn't have anyplace to be, so I had decided to sleep in and leave at checkout time.

The pounding on the door continued; I opened my eyes and glared at the hotel alarm clock. It was just after ten o'clock. The hotel maid must be knocking on the door, I decided, thinking I'd checked out.

"No, not right now," I yelled without getting out of bed. "Come back later. Checkout is at noon."

The knocking continued, more insistent now. "Come back later!" I shouted again. "Don't you see the sign on the door?"

More knocking. Grumbling, I got out of bed, yanked on my jeans and looked through the peephole.

It wasn't the maid. It was Selena.

My first thought was that something must have happened with her father. I fumbled with the lock and got the door open. "What's the matter? Why aren't you in El Paso? Don't you have a show? Did something happen?"

She was crying too hard to answer. I just held her for a while on the bed, feeling her body tremble against mine and trying to coax her to talk about whatever was going on.

Finally, Selena sat up and started telling me that she couldn't stand to be apart any longer. "I don't want anybody to be in our way," she said. "Let's get married right now."

Stunned, I just stared at her. "Wait a second. I love you. I want to be with you. You know I want to marry you someday. But why do we have to do it like this, right now?"

"There's no other way," she said, and started crying again. "We have to elope."

I felt all twisted up inside. Half of me knew that she was right, while the other half of me was worried about what she would be giving up to do this. I wanted to marry Selena. But I also understood, from being with her when she saw a wedding scene in a movie, or a picture of a bride, how much Selena had always dreamed about her glorious wedding day. She always talked about what she would do when she planned her own wedding, every detail, right down to the invitations and the cake. If we eloped, that would never happen.

"No, no, no," I told her. "I don't want to get married behind everybody's back. We can figure out a way. It's just going to take some time for your dad to get used to the idea."

"He never will," she said. "You've seen how he is!"

I kept resisting. In the back of my mind, I was terrified that if we got married in a hurry without that fairy-tale ceremony, Selena would always regret our relationship. "You've always wanted a wedding," I reminded her, smoothing her hair and pulling her closer. "I don't want to cheat you out of that white gown and the bridesmaids and the flowers. You've dreamed about it all your life. You want your family there, all around you. You want your father to walk you down the aisle."

Selena broke in, stopping me cold. "That's never going to happen, Chris."

And when she said that, I believed her. "All right," I said finally. "There is nothing that would make me happier than to marry you. What do we need to do?"

"We can go to the courthouse and get married," she said. "We can do that right now. It's the only way he'll ever leave us alone, Chris. Then we can be together."

"Okay," I said. "Let's do it. Let's get married."

I couldn't believe that those words had come out of my mouth. Married? Me? I was only twenty-two years old! But what else could I do? Selena was right. We loved each other, and there was no way that she and I were ever going to be together unless we were married. Abraham wouldn't be able to stop us from seeing each other if we were legally husband and wife. I loved the sound of that word, "wife," as I looked at Selena and repeated, "Come on. Let's go get married!"

I'll never forget Selena's smile when I said that. I could just feel all of the pressure and stress leave her body as she watched me get dressed for the courthouse. I had nothing to wear but a T-shirt and jeans; Selena was wearing a skirt and boots.

"I couldn't wear my best clothes," she admitted shyly. "Otherwise my dad would have suspected something was up."

On our second wedding anniversary, Selena and I started talking about renewing our vows after five years of marriage. We would have a real ceremony then, we promised each other. Selena bought a wedding dress and started cutting out pictures of floral arrangements she liked for our centerpieces at the reception. She even ordered a wedding registry book with a gold metal plate on it. The book had our names embossed on it, along with the date of our wedding: April 2, 1992. She had it all planned out, and it would have been a beautiful ceremony. It almost breaks my heart to think about it now.

At the Nueces County Courthouse, Selena took control and all I had to do was go with the flow. I wasn't scared, but I felt a little numb, as if I were in shock from making such an abrupt decision—one that would no doubt have consequences I couldn't even predict yet. I never would have known what to do, but Selena just kept asking questions and the clerks at the windows explained what steps we needed to take. We were lucky in that the clerk agreed to waive the standard waiting period for a marriage license—probably because nearly everyone in Corpus knew who Selena was by then.

We paid what we needed to pay, signed the necessary papers, and then stood in front of the justice of the peace, who said a few words. Then, bam, we were married, just like that. It was crazy. I couldn't believe that I was actually in this room with Selena, saying wedding vows.

Those moments went by so fast, yet I knew that the way I felt about her at that very moment was going to be the way I felt about her forever. No matter what I had thought about marriage before—not much, truthfully, given my own family history—I felt with great certainty that remembering those marriage vows would always be a sort of glue holding us together.

Neither of us cared that it was just the two of us standing in front of the justice of the peace or that we were so young. Everything else—even thoughts of the wedding Selena was giving up and worries about her father and the band—flew right out the window.

We were in love. We were husband and wife. We were happy. Nobody could come between us anymore. That's all that mattered.

The best part of the day was walking hand in hand out of the courthouse, our shoulders touching, instead of having to pull apart when we were in public. It all felt so good, even as I wondered what Abraham would do when he heard the news. Selena and I were at peace with our decision, content to know that we had finally, officially started our lives together. We had every intention of living happily ever after. Nobody could stop us from doing that now.

After the wedding, we drove straight from the courthouse in Corpus to my dad's apartment in San Antonio so that I could collect my things. San Antonio suddenly seemed safer to us since Abraham was in Corpus and we certainly weren't ready to face Selena's family with our news. Beyond that, we didn't really have a plan.

As we drove, Selena and I talked about what Abraham might do, and what would happen if he ended the band. "He's not going to do that," Selena said. "He'll come around."

Whatever we did next, from whether we lived in Corpus or San Antonio, to how we would make a living, hinged on Abraham's reaction to our wedding. We knew that we couldn't really make any decisions about anything until we talked to him.

Every now and then, Selena and I would be derailed from this logical conversation by the knowledge that we'd done it—we'd really gotten married! It was almost like having an out-of-body experience, the way we could see ourselves in the car from the outside, not quite believing that we were looking at a young couple madly, deeply in love and now—in a very weird way—on their honeymoon. We had just done something major, an act that would change our lives forever, and we were still kind of in shock because we didn't know how people would handle it.

"We're married?" one of us would ask.

"We're married!" the other would cry out, and then we'd both laugh until the tears were running down our faces.

At the same time, I tried not to imagine what Abraham and A.B. might be saying or doing right then. I was certain they'd had to cancel their gig in El Paso when Selena didn't show up, and I knew they must both be worried sick, not knowing where she was, or if she was hurt or injured. They might assume the worst; after all, Selena never spaced out or blew off a gig. She was never anything less than professional—until today. But running off to marry me was Selena's way of putting her foot down and saying "enough is enough" to her father. She was just two weeks away from her twenty-first birthday, and she was ready to assert her independence as a woman.

Selena and I kept worrying aloud about what we would do if Abraham demolished Los Dinos, but I didn't really believe that would happen. Abraham surely wouldn't throw away everything that they had worked so hard to create. I didn't know what part I'd have to play in the band, if any, but that was fine by me. I could just keep doing what I was doing, making music in San Antonio and earning my own money. I had stood up to Abraham before and I was prepared to do it again.

My father had met Selena a few times, but usually only at shows. When she came to visit me in San Antonio, we did sometimes go to the apartment, but usually during the day while my dad was at work. He liked her, though. I knew that much. Selena had that quality about her that made you feel like you'd known her forever; within minutes of seeing her, she'd joke around and make you laugh, drawing you into a conversation and making you feel comfortable. Still, growing up with Abraham, Selena had learned that fathers could be a formidable force in a family. She was extremely nervous about telling my dad our news and so was I.

When we walked into the apartment, my dad said, "Hey, what's going on?"

"Nothing much," I said, and went straight to my room to start packing, trying to think of a way to tell him. Selena, meanwhile, must have stayed in the living room; by the time I was in my room with my dad behind me, she was nowhere in sight.

That's weird, I thought, until I realized that Selena was really nervous. Even knowing her as well as I did, it always amazed me whenever Selena exhibited anxiety, because onstage she was almost another person: confident, emotional, personable, sexy, even swaggering. She always worried that people might not show up to hear her sing. Sometimes she'd peek out at the audience from backstage and, if there was a good crowd, she'd get giddy when she saw how many people were out there, no matter how popular she became. But, once Selena was in the spotlight, she gave her performances every ounce of her spirit and energy.

I started pulling clothes out of my dresser and stuffing them into a duffel bag. My father stood in the room, frowning as he watched. "*Mi hijo*, what happened?" he asked.

My father had seen me make more than one mistake—usually with cars or alcohol. He had even come to the rescue a few times. By the look on his face, I could tell that now he was really worried that I'd made another one. I said, "Nothing, Dad. Everything's fine." I swallowed hard. "But we did it."

"You did what?"

I couldn't even say the word "married." It wasn't a word that was going to just roll off my tongue. How do you go from being in a secret relationship to announcing to the world that you're married?

"We did IT," I said again.

"I still don't understand," my father said.

"Selena and I got married," I managed.

"What?" I had a chair in my room that I used to sit in to practice guitar. Now Dad sat down really slowly on that chair and shook his head.

I could tell that, for him, this wasn't bad news, exactly, but it wasn't good news, either. "Damn," he said.

My father, always ready for a conversation, was nearly speechless. As I stood there watching him, I realized why: After being in a marriage that didn't work out, after struggling to create relationships with kids he never lived with, my father knew that marrying young, or marrying at any age, wasn't always going to end up the way you thought it might.

"Man," he said now, clenching his fists a little. "Why did Abraham have to push you like that? What did he think was going to happen?"

"It's okay, Dad," I reassured him. "It's a good thing. Everything is cool."

A sudden movement in the doorway made me glance in that direction. Selena was standing there now, looking in, her brown eyes so huge that it was almost comical.

My father turned around and slowly got to his feet when he saw Selena. Then he took a couple of steps toward her, and Selena rushed into his arms, where he folded her into a great hug.

We sat and talked with my father for a while, and then we drove over to my mom's. I'm not sure what possessed Selena and me to go there, of all places, for our wedding night. I guess we were both feeling pretty shaky and just needed to be someplace where we knew we would be accepted as who we were: newlyweds who had just promised to love, honor, and cherish one another for a lifetime. Nothing more, and certainly nothing less.

At any rate, we drove to my mother's house and told her and Pops the news. Again, I had trouble getting the words out.

"Mom, we did it," I said.

"What did you do?" she asked, looking from Selena to me.

"You know, Mom. The 'M' word."

As close as she was to my mother, Selena must have been really nervous here, too, for she suddenly announced, "I have to go to the bathroom," and fled.

My mother and stepfather reacted to our news much the same way my dad had. They knew how in love we were, and they were happy to hear that we were married. But they both thought it was a shame that Selena and I had been driven to marry so young, and in secret.

Finally, in bed that night, Selena and I talked about what might happen next. We agreed to live in Selena's apartment in Corpus—a place that she had been using as a studio of sorts for her fashion design hobby—as long as her father didn't harass us once we started living there.

"You're coming back to the band," Selena said. She was asking me and telling me at the same time.

"No," I told her. "No way. After everything I've been through with your father and Los Dinos, I have no desire to deal with that stuff."

She sat up in bed next to me. "What are you talking about? It's not going to be like that."

"You don't know what's going to happen," I said. "Neither of us knows what Abraham will do."

She didn't like hearing that. But it was true. I wasn't about to drop what I was doing to run back to the band. I was pretty convinced that I'd be better off on my own than with Los Dinos.

Suddenly, my mother's house phone rang. It was A.B. The family had been trying to track down Selena all day, he said, and they knew about our marriage.

Today, of course, people would have been tweeting or texting or blogging about it before she and I even made it out of the courthouse. Even without all that, news of our marriage had spread within the hour. The clerks at City Hall had probably told their friends, "Hey, guess who got a marriage license today?" This gossip had led people in the music business to catch wind of it. DJs started phoning Abraham's house to see if the news was true. A few radio stations even announced the news.

Selena's face paled when she first started talking to her brother and discovered that everyone in her family knew about our marriage by now. Then, all of a sudden, her brother said something that made her laugh. That was a good sign, I thought, feeling my stomach unclench a little.

Suddenly, Selena thrust the phone in my direction. "A.B. wants to talk to you," she said.

My first reaction was to say no. But Selena gave me this look, and I knew I didn't have any choice.

A.B. has a quality that he shared with Selena, an ability to disarm you within seconds of starting up a conversation, no matter how set you might be against him. He did that with me now.

As soon as I got on the phone, A.B. said, "Welcome to the family, bro," and then he was laughing and I couldn't help it. I started laughing, too, because the whole situation seemed so surreal. Plus, A.B. and I had started out as friends long before I became involved with his little sister. As tough as I wanted to be with him, as much as I wanted to hang on to my anger because everyone in the band had turned their backs on me, when I heard A.B say those words, my anger just melted away. Gone.

We talked a little more, and A.B. did apologize at last. "Man, I'm sorry things went the way they did," he said. "But it's all right now. Y'all are married, and it's for the best. You're coming on the road with us, right?"

The question caught me off guard. "Well," I said, trying to think past the shocks that just kept coming. "Do you all want me to come back?"

"Of course," he said. "Who else can play guitar like you can?"

"Is your dad cool with that?" I asked.

"He's going to have to accept it," A.B. said. "He's a little upset right now. He's not taking the news very well, but he'll get used to the idea."

Of course that wasn't quite what I wanted to hear. But what else had I expected? "All right," I said. "If you say it's cool, then I'll come back."

"I do. Tell my sister that I love her and I'll see you guys soon," A.B. said. "Welcome to the family, brother-in-law."

We both started laughing again, and then I hung up. Selena had been listening to all of this, of course. If she had been happy before, now she was ecstatic. Everything was falling into place just as she had hoped.

We fell back into bed and wrapped our arms around each other, still amazed at our good fortune: We had found each other and our love had proved stronger than any obstacles thrown our way.

SIX

OUR FIRST MONTHS AS MAN AND WIFE

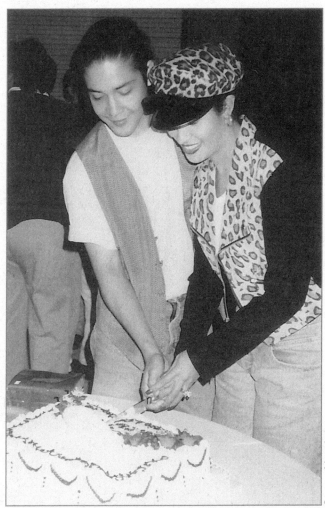

The next day, Selena and I moved into her apartment in Corpus and started our honeymoon. Her father showed up at our door hours after we'd arrived.

Abraham's expression was unreadable. I felt my hands go cold and my heart started pounding. I was determined to be civil—this was Selena's father, after all—but I wasn't about to invite him inside. How could I trust this man, who had done nothing but hurl insults at me since finding out that I loved his daughter?

The worst-scase scenario, as I saw it, was that Abraham would accept me, without really accepting me, if you know what I mean. Maybe he would invite me into the band again to keep Selena happy, but there was a good possibility that he might act like I was family when Selena was around, but otherwise make it clear that he was still displeased—clear enough that the other band members might continue giving me the cold shoulder. I was therefore polite when Abraham arrived, but reserved; I no longer trusted the man any more than he trusted me.

Selena stayed inside the apartment while Abraham and I talked outside. I never thought to ask her later if she'd known Abraham was coming over. He did that often after we were married—just dropped by unannounced—so she may have had no idea that Abraham was on his way.

I had been expecting the worst, so I was surprised when Abraham held things together. He didn't say anything derogatory. In fact, he even began with an apology. If he'd been wearing a hat, he might have even taken it off and twisted it in his hands.

"I shouldn't have been the way that I was," he said. "I hope you know that I was only protecting Selena."

I told him that I did know that, but I was still offended and hurt. "When we were on the road together, I spent more time with you and your family than I did with my own family," I pointed out. "You should know me by now. I would never do anything to hurt Selena. I love her."

He nodded, accepting this, it seemed. Then Abraham became businesslike—the mode he was most comfortable in, I knew. "Are you coming back to the band?" he asked.

I could have taken a stance and resisted—not just to be contrary, but because I truly was happy playing around San Antonio with Rudy and Albert, and working as an independent musician. Did I really want all of the baggage that would come with rejoining Los Dinos and the Quintanilla family?

Again, though, I tried to see things from Abraham's point of view. He must have been humiliated and angry when he heard that Selena and I had gotten married behind his back. Because he had no idea of the true nature of our relationship, and didn't even know how long we had been seeing each other, it must have been a total shock when strangers telephoned to tell him that his beloved youngest daughter, who in his eyes had the potential to be a superstar, had gone against his wishes and married a long-haired guitarist whom he didn't deem worthy.

I decided that if Selena's father could behave so professionally with all of his emotions surely swirling around inside him, I could, too. Plus I knew how happy Selena would be if I rejoined Los Dinos. "I'll come back if you want me to," I said. "It's up to you and A.B."

"Selena wants you in the group," Abraham said gruffly, and then he actually gave me a hug. He was shaking a little with emotion.

Feeling the tremor in his body, I realized, once again, how devastated Abraham must have been when he discovered that Selena had gone against his wishes, and how much it had cost him to come over here and accept me into the family. Selena was his baby girl, and I know that man loved her more than his own life. But Abraham had apologized and he was trying to make it possible for us to have a relationship both within the family and in the band. I respected him for that.

We went into the apartment together then. Selena and Abraham hugged each other for a long time. She started crying, and then Abraham did, too.

"I'm sorry I pushed you kids into a corner," Abraham said at last. "Let's just continue from here. We'll go on doing what we were doing as a band, and we'll move forward over this bump in the road."

So we embraced, said our apologies, and agreed to move on. It was a good thing we did, too, because things were ready to explode on the music scene for Selena y Los Dinos.

To celebrate our love, I decided to pay a special tribute to Selena with my favorite guitar. The guitar was a white Jackson Soloist. It was the first electric guitar I had ever bought that was considered top-of-the-line, and it did everything I needed it to do. Even when I upgraded to a Fender Stratocaster, I kept the Jackson with me as a backup guitar onstage and still played it now and then.

One night, Selena and I were doing a show in Austin when my good friend Tony Gonzales stopped by. Tony was an artist; he had designed and painted a number of shirts for me. When he came by the bus after the show, he brought me a T-shirt with a portrait of Selena on it, and that gave me an idea. I had always wanted a guitar with artwork on it, but I didn't want anything mass produced. I also wanted to choose artwork that really symbolized something important in my life.

"Hey, Tony," I said, "can you paint on my guitar?"

He looked startled. "Dude, yeah, I can paint on anything. But that's your guitar, man."

"I know. But I really want you to do this thing for me." I told him that I wanted him to paint a portrait of Selena right on the Jackson's white face. When Tony agreed, I started taking the guitar apart right there on the bus.

Selena came by and saw me in the bus with this stranger. I had a screwdriver in my hand, and the Jackson was in pieces all over the bus table. Selena gasped. "Chris, what happened to your guitar?"

I introduced her to Tony, and said, "Tony's a real good friend of mine, and he's an artist. We go way back. Here, look." I showed her the shirt Tony had painted.

"You did that?" Selena examined the shirt, clearly impressed.

"Yeah," Tony said. He's a shy person and never would have shown her anything. But he was pleased by her reaction.

"I'm going to have him paint a picture on my guitar," I said.

Selena just stared at me like I'd gone insane. "Are you sure?"

"Yeah, I'm sure."

Tony said, "So what do you want, Chris?" He already knew that I wanted a portrait of Selena. He also knew enough not to tell her.

"Surprise me," I said. "Just do what you do."

"What's he going to paint on there?" Selena asked.

"Oh, it's just going to be a black-and-white picture. Nothing major." By now, I had the guitar face off. I handed it to Tony and stored all of the little metal bits and strings in a plastic bag.

The next time we played in Austin, Tony brought back my guitar with this gorgeous picture of Selena on it. I put the guitar back together in secret, while Selena was busy getting dressed for the show, and then I just carried the Jackson out to the stage and set it on the stand as my backup guitar.

When she came out, I said, "Here. Check out what Tony did." I pointed at the Jackson.

Selena covered her mouth and her eyes went wide. She was all smiles and totally tripping. "I can't believe you did that for me!"

"See? I told you Tony's a great artist," I said.

Selena loved that guitar. To be honest, I felt a little weird playing the Jackson at first, because our marriage was still so new, but after a while I was very proud of it. The fans loved the guitar, too; they would take pictures of me playing it, or just photos of the guitar on its stand.

At the same time that Tony brought over my Jackson, he gave Selena and me a gift: a three foot by four foot painting of Selena's face and hand that he had done in black, gray, and white. The painting fit our art deco décor perfectly. We hung it above the couch, between a pair of tall floor lamps with smoky glass bowls. When we turned the fader switch down on the lights, Selena's face was the only thing you could see in the living room. I still treasure that painting.

In the Tejano world, groups knocked out their albums fast. We were no exception. The Quintanilla family had an incredible work ethic, and I continued learning a lot from A.B. We could put together an album in a month or less, and that included writing the songs out of thin air as well as arranging, producing, and recording them.

There are very simple ways to play Tejano music, but we were continuing to incorporate new sounds. I was a good enough guitar player that I could play broken chords, sustained notes, and a lot of different rhythms. Even though we were playing within a certain genre, I was like A.B., in the sense that I wanted to think outside the box and do something different.

Basically, anytime we were ready to make an album, we'd book the studio for a week and record the whole album at once. In the weeks leading up to that, we spent time perfecting the songs in A.B.'s bedroom studio—he lived in a house next to Abraham. At the studio, instrumental and vocal tracks had to be recorded separately and from beginning to end before they could be mixed. If you messed one of those up, you had to go back in and start over.

During my first year with Los Dinos, we had released an album comprised of Selena's old songs because Capitol EMI had bought them from the previous label and they wanted them rerecorded. For that album, we recorded the songs exactly as they had been written originally. I simply played the same guitar part that had already been done before. I wasn't the kind of guy who was going to try to take over; I was being as true as I could be to the guitar sounds they'd had on those songs originally, to the point that most people probably didn't even realize it was a different guitar player.

But, in creating *Entre a Mi Mundo* in 1992, we broke out of that mold and came up with truly innovative sounds. The album shot to the top of the charts and went gold fast. My favorite song on the album, "Como La Flor," was written by Pete and A.B. while we were on Big Bertha touring in late 1991. The song's simple, plaintive melody and aching lyrics tell the story of someone who sees her old love with someone new and must move on; she wishes him the best and compares their love to a flower that has withered and died.

"Como La Flor" was the first solo song of Selena's to really take off, especially in Mexico. The song became a fan favorite and one of Selena's signature songs. Selena really loved to sing all of the songs we did, but "Como La Flor" was probably her favorite. As it gained popularity, we began either opening or closing our sets with that particular song, with fans singing along to the chorus, *"Ay, ay, ay, como me duele."* The bigger that song got, the greater our connection was with the crowd.

Even though I love "Como La Flor," I don't think it would have been such a popular song if Selena hadn't been the one singing it. The lyrics and music aren't what make the song special; it's the emotion in Selena's voice. Every time she sang "Como La Flor," that emotion came through and it was real. I've heard a lot of people sing it since, but nobody can touch people's hearts with that song the way Selena did.

Entre a Mi Mundo propelled us to another level in the music business entirely. The album was number one on Billboard's Regional Mexican Album's chart and was called the number one Regional Mexican Album of the Year. More importantly, this album made it onto the Top Latin 50 chart.

We had done it. EMI now considered us a commercial group. It was one of the happiest times in my life: I was making music, Selena and I were married and still madly in love, and the band was poised to enter the international market. Of course, because every one of us had come up from hard times, we never let our successes go to our heads and took nothing for granted—especially Abraham.

"We have a number one hit? So what?" Abraham would say. "Any clown can get to number one. The question is, can you do it again?"

We didn't know. But we were sure going to try—Selena harder than anyone.

It helped that we were in the right place at the right time. Latin music seemed to be everywhere that year, playing on radios all across the U.S. and not just in our corner of the southwest. *Billboard* magazine had even started "Hot Latin Songs," which tracked Latin music in the American music market. This chart was based on airplay on Spanish-language radio stations, but the songs didn't have to be in Spanish. Selena's idol, Rocio Durcal, put out the first song to reach number one on that chart, "La Guirnalda." Since then, the chart had featured hits by Chayanne, Luis Miguel, Marco Antonio Solis, Ana Gabriel, Gloria Estefan, and Selena herself, whose duet with Alvaro Torres, "Buenos Amigos," hit number one the year we were married.

Within this mix, Selena y Los Dinos were representing regional Mexican or Tejano music, but in a completely new and different light. We were striving to set ourselves apart from other groups in the Tejano world. We weren't those guys wearing cowboy hats,

Wrangler jeans, and boots. None of the other Tejano bands were as young as we were. Besides being young, we were all incredibly energetic, talented, and willing to do whatever it took to create a unique sound.

Ricky Vela was writing creative songs with heavy arrangements. I brought in the rock and roll element because I had been in a Top 40 cover band and I loved experimenting on the guitar. Joe, our keyboardist, was raised in the border town of Laredo, so he brought that traditional street music. Pete, our other singer and songwriter, brought in complex lyrics and melodies with lots of chords. A.B. held down the bass line and arranged our songs to highlight Selena's vocals, and Selena put her soul into singing. We were poised and ready to cross over into the international music scene like Gloria Estefan.

Soon after Selena and I were married, the band was invited to perform in Las Vegas at the Premio Lo Nuestro awards for Latin musicians, sponsored by *Billboard*. This was the first hint I had of the fame that would soon come barreling our way.

Something was wrong with Big Bertha, so we all piled into a fifteen-passenger van and drove nonstop to Las Vegas from Corpus. This wasn't the most comfortable way to ride fourteen hundred miles, but as always, the cool thing about Los Dinos was that all of us were determined to do whatever it took to propel our music to the top of the charts. We never complained. We just did what we needed to do, especially Selena.

We arrived at Caesars Palace at about ten o'clock in the morning. I couldn't believe that I was in this city that I had always heard so much about, but had seen only on TV and in the movies. The sight of so many neon signs had me reeling. The lights, the smells, the sounds of the coins dropping in the slot machines—it was almost too much stimulation for me to handle.

I'll never forget checking into our suite at the Palace with Selena. Not because it was a cool room—though it was! Really, it wouldn't have mattered to me if they'd given us a matchbox-size room in the basement. It was just such a joy to have our relationship out in the open, and to hear people say, "Well, they're married, so they should get the suite." We were finally able to be on our own without having to think of excuses or sneak around behind Abraham's back.

Selena and I lay down and slept for a little while, trying to recover from the long drive. I was so excited to be in Las Vegas, though, that I soon got up and went downstairs by myself to play the slot machines.

Within an hour, I had hit and won enough quarters to fill up my little white plastic cup. I was so excited that I walked as fast as I could back to the elevator. I couldn't wait to show my big winnings to Selena!

Back in the room, I dumped the quarters on the bed and started counting them. I was convinced that I'd won at least a thousand bucks, the cup was that heavy. It turned out to be maybe sixty dollars in all.

Selena laughed, but when she saw my crestfallen expression, she said, "Come on. Let's go back down there. I'll show you how it's done." She put on her clothes and we went downstairs.

"Are you crazy?" I asked when Selena got one hundred dollars in dollar coins.

"Just watch," she said. "If you see somebody playing a slot machine but not winning anything, it's starting to get hot. We'll go play it as soon as that person leaves."

Finally, we spotted a guy who had been playing on the same slot machine who just kept losing and losing. The minute he left, Selena said, "Okay. Let's go get it."

We walked over to the machine and started feeding it coins. Selena went to put three dollars in, and when I tried to stop her, freaking out over that, too, she said, "If you put in just one dollar at a time, you don't get as much as if you put in three."

"Wait, that's a lot of money," I protested. I still couldn't get my head around this whole concept of possibly losing so much money. Then again, I never was the kind of risk taker Selena was all her life.

"Shhh," Selena said. "Just push this button here so it spins, and I'll do the lever thing."

We did that three times, and that's all it took. The machine started spitting dollar coins, and before I knew it, we had three hundred dollars in our hands.

After playing the slots for a little while longer, Selena said, "Let's go play blackjack!"

"You're crazy," I said. "I am not sitting at one of those tables and losing money. I don't know anything about playing blackjack."

"Come on, it's easy," she pleaded.

"No, no, no," I said.

"What's the matter?" she teased. "Can't you count fast enough?"

I folded my arms. "Say what you want. I'm not playing."

Selena laughed. "Okay, then. Watch what I do. If you want to do it, just jump in."

So I watched, and again, Selena amazed me. I have no idea if she'd ever played blackjack before or if, once again, she just put her mind to something and learned it faster than anybody else could have. Selena sat down at one of those blackjack tables and, within minutes, she had mastered all of the hand signals. She tapped on the table or waved her hand over her cards, and even slid her cards under the chips when she wanted to stand.

Selena lost a few hands and, quickly disgusted with herself, said, "Let's go."

But she hated to lose at anything, so I knew that wasn't the end of it. Sure enough, Selena returned to that same table a little while later, sat down, and played a few more hands until she started winning. Then, smiling that full-wattage smile of hers, she said, "All right. I'm out."

She didn't care about the money. She just wanted to know that she could win.

At the Vegas show, I realized for the first time that we had been big fish in the small Tejano pond, but now we were swimming in a much bigger pond with more exotic fish. Our old friends La Mafia were there; that group now included my friend Rudy on bass, so it was a bit of a reunion for us.

I was hanging with those guys while Selena went off to do some shopping with Suzette, when all of a sudden I saw Ricky Martin heading toward us. He was just making his name as a solo artist after a huge career with the group Menudo.

"Hey, I like your work. What's going on?" Ricky said. As we stood there talking, I realized with amazement that musicians I admired were actually listening to our songs.

In addition to performing at the *Billboard* show, we walked away with the regional Mexican music award and it became clear to all of us that we were achieving our goal of having our music recognized internationally. It was time to cross the border and play in Mexico and Latin America—the next logical step before we broke into the mainstream English market.

SEVEN

MAKING MUSIC IN MEXICO

AP Photo / *Houston Chronicle*, Dave Einrel

The promoters at Capitol EMI were intent on having us continue building our reputation on the international music scene after the success of *Entre a Mi Mundo*. This meant traveling abroad.

Mexico was the logical place to begin our international publicity blitz. We already had a fan base there, and we could easily drive to the shows from Texas. Of course, none of us fully realized just how nerve-racking it would be to go from playing relatively small venues in the U.S. to playing large amphitheaters and doing interviews in Spanish in Mexico.

We were scheduled to play in Monterrey during our first trip, and there was mad press all day. We went from one interview to the next: radio, television, magazine journalists, you name it. Before the trip, Rick had helped me practice saying my name and what instrument I played.

I kept repeating this phrase to myself like a mantra: "*Mi nombre es Chris Perez y toco la guitarra. Mi nombre es Chris Perez y toco la guitarra.*" I knew how absurd the Mexican journalists would think it was if we sang in Spanish but couldn't even manage to speak in basic textbook phrases. I was determined not to embarrass the band—or myself.

Despite my good intentions and all of that practicing, I still managed to humiliate myself. During our first interview with the radio DJs in Monterrey, we all had to go down the line and introduce ourselves, just as we'd practiced. I froze up completely. When it was my turn, I said *"toca"* instead of *"toco,"* essentially saying, "My name is Chris Perez and he plays the guitar." Naturally, everyone laughed at my expense.

"Dude, I told you how to say it," Ricky scolded me afterward.

"I know, I know," I said miserably.

My only source of comfort was that some of the other band members stumbled around in Spanish, too. Selena, though, rose to the challenge, as she always did. She was the one who really felt the media pressure, because by now everyone in Mexico knew her not only from her music, but from the Coca-Cola commercials. She was already hugely popular in that country and crowds surrounded us everywhere we went, to the point where Selena couldn't even get off the bus unless it was to duck into a hotel or go onstage.

With the journalists, Selena was as personable as ever, giving each media personality a warm hug and a big smile, winning them over before she ever had to say a word. As a third-generation Texan who had to learn Spanish phonetically, with her father coaching her on her accent, she knew that there was a chance that the Mexican fans might dismiss her. Instead, they adored everything about her, from her dark hair and brown eyes to her curvy figure.

The fans saw Selena's sincerity and generosity, and felt her love for them. Selena appealed to everyone from excitable preteen girls who wanted to dress and dance like her, to *abuelas* who loved those heart-wrenching ballads like "Como La Flor."

To Mexicans, and to most Mexican-Americans, Selena was that perfect symbol: a sexy star who had come up from the streets, bringing her family with her, and still remaining virtuous and hardworking along the way. It wasn't an act, either. What they saw was true and the fans knew that.

In Mexico, Selena mangled her conversations in Spanish like the rest of us, but not for long. She said, "It'll be cool. You watch. I'm going to learn Spanish and surprise everybody."

Every minute we were in Mexico, Selena's Spanish jumped up a notch. She got better and better, to the point where I'd have to ask her to slow down so that I could understand what she was saying. Her fluency in Spanish eventually helped her in Los Angeles and Miami as well as in Mexico, because at those concerts the audience was also made up mostly of Spanish-speaking fans who all wanted to hear her music. They came from Mexico, Cuba, Puerto Rico, you name it: the accents were all different, but everyone loved Selena.

It was in Mexico where we had the craziest, most zealous fans. They showed up in numbers we rarely saw at concerts in the U.S., and although we appreciated how completely they had embraced us, sometimes it was overwhelming.

For instance, during one tour in Monterrey, we were playing to tens of thousands of people in an outdoor arena. Suddenly the crowd—too many people, packed in too closely beneath an intensely hot sun, without water or shade—started surging forward. The audience members shoved and pushed against each other as a force of energy moved the crowd forward. People were getting trampled below the stage. Others were climbing up the scaffolding, trying to get to us, especially to Selena.

"Get out of here!" Abraham barked at us. "Now!" He motioned for us to run for the bus, which was parked right behind the stage.

Hearts pounding, we did as we were ordered, leaving Abraham out there to try to intimidate the crowd, make them behave.

Whatever he said didn't work. The audience started throwing half-empty beer cans at the instruments, equipment, and speakers, the metallic sounds ringing like gunshot even above the noise of people chanting and shouting for us to return.

The arena was enclosed by high walls. There was really only one way in and one way out; all I could think about was what might happen next if the fans rushed around the stage, dodged the barricades, and surrounded our bus. I put my arm around Selena and eyed the height of the wall, considering whether we could manage to jump over it if we climbed on top of the bus.

Finally, Selena shook me off. As daring and courageous as she was, she wasn't about to just sit there. She knew that the fans were only impatient because they couldn't see her. She went out onstage and faced the mob. Speaking in Spanish, she asked them to please calm down so that she could sing to them.

The fans always listened to her. They quieted and we went back onstage, fingers crossed that we'd be able to get out of that arena in one piece.

That was how it was in Mexico: exciting, thrilling, and a little scary. We all had to learn as we went—including our promoters. Fame had come to us before we were quite ready for it.

Anytime we played in Monterrey, it was especially crazy, because people here had been listening to Selena's music from across the border long before she ever came to Mexico. Not only did we do interviews all day, we'd also do afternoon and evening shows. We wouldn't get a lot of sleep, so everyone was irritable. We didn't even have time to get out and walk around or see anything of the city. We were too busy doing promotional stops for Capitol EMI.

We were sent from one building to the next, sometimes stopping in a building that had three or four different radio stations in it to do interviews. Then off we'd go to squeeze in a TV show. If we were hungry, we'd hit a drive-through McDonald's, or maybe we'd get lucky and have half an hour to stop at a seafood place.

Selena wasn't able to go into those restaurants with us, though, because she was always recognized. Even Ricky, Joe, and I sometimes had trouble. The road crew might be sitting at a table in a restaurant, just relaxing, and then we'd come in and you could see them tense right up because they knew the potential was there for fans to start crowding around the table once they saw us.

We were increasingly popular in the U.S., but in Mexico there was such a constant media storm that the number of fans continued to escalate by the thousands. Our names and photographs appeared in so many magazines that we'd come out of a TV studio or a radio station and have to run to the safety of our two Suburbans as we traveled from one interview to the next.

We did have security guards, but they were there to protect Selena. For the rest of us, it was every man for himself. I was really scared a few times that I would get left behind while the Suburbans roared out of the crowd, but your adrenaline is so high in a situation like that, you just kick into survival mode.

I remember making one particular trek through a crowd wearing a jacket studded with rhinestones. As I ran for the car, a fan tried to grab on to my jacket; there was a big hole in the jacket by the time I made it into the backseat, because the fan had ripped a rhinestone right off. Another time, I had a three-hundred-dollar pair of sunglasses yanked right off my face.

None of this was as bad for me as it was for Selena, though. Even in the U.S., she could hardly leave the bus now. I could step outside and breathe some fresh air. Selena couldn't do that or she'd be mobbed.

Sometimes, I'd be talking to somebody on the sidewalk below and Selena would open the back window of the bus and start joking around with us. But there was always somebody who seemed to know where we were. We'd hear a shout from up the street, "There's Selena!" and I'd have to yell at her to make sure the bus windows and door were all tightly closed.

I had another big worry. Oscar Flores, the promoter of our Mexican tour, had insisted that I was to be introduced only as the band's guitarist. "You and Selena can't tell anyone you're married," he said. "It'll ruin her image."

I didn't feel right about lying to the fans. Plus, it was already difficult enough for me sometimes to believe that we were truly married. For many weeks after the wedding, I couldn't escape that subterfuge mentality I'd been living with for so long. As it was, I still sometimes walked about two feet away from Selena instead of holding her hand like any other newlywed husband might do.

Selena didn't like the idea of lying about our marriage either, but Abraham, too, counseled us that this might be the better public image to maintain. He was afraid the fans might not like the idea of a married woman being a lead singer, and it might tarnish Selena's image as a fresh young talent if she were coupled with someone like me.

Reluctantly, Selena and I agreed at first not to discuss our relationship in public. We knew we were playing in a brand-new game with a new set of rules, and we thought Oscar and Abraham might be right.

Because that time predated Internet news and social media, it was possible to keep our marriage a secret despite the fact that Corpus was so close to Monterrey. Nonetheless, a few rumors continued to circulate about Selena being married. Some people even thought that she must have married Pete, since he sang so many duets with her and they often danced together onstage.

At one point, a journalist asked Selena point blank if she had a boyfriend, and she had to say, "No," which cut me to the quick. But I went along with it. I understood that the music business was partly about image, and I was willing to do whatever it took to get Selena in front of as many people as possible.

When journalists asked the rest of us if anyone was married or had a girlfriend, we'd all point to A.B., who had been married to his wife Vangie for a while by then and sometimes brought her on tour with his kids. The rest of us came up with pat answers like, "Me? My girlfriend is this band!"

The knowledge that we were hiding our marriage—and our sacred wedding vows—kept eating away at Selena. After a few trips to Mexico, she put a stop to the lies.

"I'm proud to be married to Chris, and I want to tell the world," she told Abraham when he argued. "Besides, how's it going to look to our fans if we keep hiding this? It's only a two-hour drive between Corpus and Monterrey. Somebody's going to find out, and then it's going to look really bad."

From then on, she started saying "yes" to the journalists who asked if rumors that she'd been married were true, and the news seemed only to increase her fans' affection and admiration.

In the States, too, she talked happily to reporters about our marriage. She even talked about it when I would rather she didn't, because I was basically such a private person. At one concert, for instance, she went around introducing all of her band members to the audience as she always did: "This is my brother A.B. on bass, this is my sister Suzette on drums," and so forth. I don't know what clued me in, but I knew that Selena was going to introduce me differently on that particular day.

Don't do it, don't do it, don't embarrass me, I telegraphed silently. I was still shy about openly discussing our relationship, I suppose because Selena was such a public figure, and I didn't want people to think I'd married her for any of the wrong reasons—such as fame, sex appeal, or money—as I knew most people would speculate.

Selena tortured me by introducing me last. Then, sure enough, she said, "Last but not least, on the guitar, give it up for my husband, Chris Perez!"

The guys in the audience started booing at this, but Selena just laughed. She wasn't fazed by their reaction at all. "Oh, come on, if I were married to any of you, you know you wouldn't be booing!" she said, and at that, everybody went crazy and started laughing, including me.

EIGHT

BLISS, MOSTLY

A month or so into our marriage, I came home one night to find the apartment dark but for a few candles placed here and there. No music played. The television was off.

"Selena?" I called anxiously.

"Here."

I turned and saw her then, sitting on the couch in the cool darkness. Beyond, the table was set for dinner and something smelled good in the kitchen. "You did all this for me?" I asked.

"For us," she said.

"What, is it an anniversary I don't know about?" I teased.

"It's for us, that's all," she said.

We sat down at the table across from each other, and Selena served the meal. But we didn't really eat, because we started talking so deeply about our feelings.

"I love you, Christopher," Selena said. She always used my full name whenever things were serious or intense between us. "Let's never let anything between us change. Promise?" Her voice was as solemn as I'd ever heard it.

"I promise," I said, and told her how much I loved her, too. "I don't know what I'd do if I ever lost you," I confessed.

Selena was the first person who had ever gotten me to feel this deeply about anyone or anything. I know that she felt the same way about me. Suddenly, we were both crying, weeping silent, slow tears of joy because we had been lucky enough to find each other, and we knew that we were going to be together forever.

We laughed about it afterward, a little. But we both knew that something magical had happened. Not many people on this earth get to feel what we did. Our love for each other went even more deeply than the bonds of marriage.

Selena had originally rented her apartment in Corpus principally to use as a studio and workspace. Most of the space was dominated by a huge table where Selena did all of her fashion sketches and clothing designs. She also made some of her own clothes there; that girl could do more with rhinestones and a bra than anyone.

Music was Selena's business, but her real passion was for clothes. She was becoming increasingly passionate about opening her own fashion boutique someday. This wasn't because she needed the money, but because she loved clothes more than just about anything, and she wanted something in her life that was all her own.

"When I get my hair and nails done, I've got to pay for it," Selena would joke. "I might as well buy my own boutique and salon so that I can get that done for free whenever I want."

Unlike the rest of Selena's family, who scoffed at the idea of her actually going through with this fantasy of someday opening a fashion boutique and salon, I loved fantasizing with her about doing that. I could see how important the idea was to her.

I understood that Selena desperately needed an independent, creative outlet—something that wasn't about her family or even about making music. The business of being an increasingly popular entertainer was starting to wear on her. Selena was typically upbeat, energetic, and ready to do whatever was asked of her on behalf of the band. But, as things heated up and she felt more pressure, she occasionally broke down and cried for no apparent reason. This frightened me because I had no idea what to do when that happened.

The first time I ever witnessed one of Selena's emotional low points was terrifying, because it was clear evidence of how fragile she really was, and of how much strain she was feeling as the lead singer for Los Dinos and as an entertainer who was beginning to gain momentum internationally. It also frightened me because I didn't know how to help her.

It happened about a month after Selena and I were married. We were going through our CDs in the living room when Selena found *Revenge*, one of my Kiss albums.

"What's this?" she asked, holding it up and making a face at the cover.

"That's Kiss," I said. "Check it out." I had been a huge Kiss fan since childhood, I told her, and my bedroom as a teenager had once been papered in Kiss posters, even on the ceiling.

I tried to talk to her about why I liked this group's music so much, but Selena wouldn't listen. This was rare for her; usually she was open-minded about being introduced to any kind of new music, no matter what genre.

"I don't want this CD in the house," Selena announced.

"Are you serious?" I asked in disbelief.

"Yes," she said. "You have to get rid of it."

"But why?"

Selena held the CD at arm's length, as if it stank. "It's the cover," she said. "I hate it. It's wicked."

I frowned at the album cover, which had a gray background and "Kiss" printed in tall black letters, with the word "Revenge" written in what was supposed to look like red blood. It might not have been a pretty cover, but it was striking, and there wasn't anything particularly horrible about it. "I think you're tripping," I said.

Somehow, the conversation blew up into a big argument, since I couldn't believe Selena would be that irrational, and Selena was being as stubborn as always, insisting that I toss that album cover out immediately.

Finally, I said, "All right. Okay, already! I'll keep the album, but I'll just take the cover and throw it out! Will you be satisfied then?"

At that, Selena started crying. Not sniffling, either, but sobbing hard and starting to shake. That's when I knew that our argument wasn't just about a CD.

"What is it?" I asked gently. "Talk to me."

Selena tried to speak, but I couldn't understand what she was saying, she was crying so hard. She had been standing up and leaning against the wall; now she slowly started sliding down to the floor.

What was going on? I had no idea. All I could think to do was grab her and hold her.

I held Selena close for a long time, saying, "I'm sorry, I'm sorry."

For what, I didn't know, but I kept saying it over and over again until she calmed down.

More often than I liked, I was caught between Selena and Abraham. Occasionally I got the raw end of the deal, like the time we were returning from playing at the Colorado State Fair.

It was late at night and we knew we had a long drive ahead of us. By then, we had a crew, a security guy, and a driver for the bus. Everything was in place for us to leave except, of course, Selena. I had gone back to the hotel room to check to see if she was ready to leave, but of course she wasn't.

"Go back in there and get her to come out," Abraham commanded.

I did as I was told. "Hey, everybody is at the bus waiting for you," I said.

"Tell Dad to hold his horses. I'll be there in a few minutes," Selena said. "Can you carry this bag out for me and send somebody back for the rest of my stuff?"

I returned to the bus—a much nicer one now than our old tour bus, Big Bertha—and informed Abraham that it would be a few minutes yet before Selena was ready, but somebody from the road crew could go collect her bags.

Abraham was standing halfway up the bus steps. The rest of the band and the crew were there as well, just sitting in the front of the bus and watching. Abraham gave me a really nasty look, and I thought, *Oh, man. Why am I in the middle of this crap? I've had enough of this guy. I don't deserve to be treated this way.*

Out of respect for Selena's father, though, I held my temper. I walked past him and everyone else to put some of Selena's gear in her bunk.

"Where's Selena?" Abraham snapped. "Why isn't she out here with the rest of us?"

I worked to keep my voice calm. "I told you. She said that somebody can come out and get her stuff. She's a grown-up woman, Abraham. She'll be here when she's ready."

Abraham shot the rest of the way up the bus steps, making a lot of noise, and barreled down the hallway toward me. Startled, I took a step back. I had no idea what Abraham was going to do. I didn't want to hit him, but I wanted to be ready in case he hit me. I stood perfectly still and let him come at me. I could have pushed him or fought him, and believe me, I thought about it.

Then I stopped myself. What was I doing?

Abraham pulled himself together, too. He slammed shut the door to the bunk room so that nobody else could see us, and gave me a hug. "Sorry, son," he said. "I'm just in a bad mood because I'm in a hurry."

"It's cool, it's cool," I said, and that was that.

Or so I thought. I have no idea what Abraham told Selena about this incident to save face, but it must have been some version that made me into the bad guy, because she was angry at me for days.

"You need to apologize for what you did to him," she lectured.

"He's the one who needed to apologize, and he did!" I argued.

"You disrespected him, Chris, and he's my father," she said. "I can't let you do that."

I refused. But Selena gave me the cold shoulder from that moment on, and her will was usually stronger than anybody's. By the third day, I was sick of the whole stupid argument. I realized that it wouldn't cost me that much to apologize—and it would make Selena happy.

So I went up to Abraham and said, "I'm sorry for the other night. I shouldn't have gone there. Nothing like that should have happened between us." I deliberately left the apology vague because, although I was definitely sorry that things had gotten to that point between us, I knew I hadn't done anything wrong.

Abraham, though, got this maddening little smirk on his face, as if he thought he'd won somehow. Then he opened his arms and gave me one of his famous hugs.

Another time, an argument started up between Selena and her dad in the kitchen while I was in the living room. He had just stopped by, unannounced, the way he loved to do, and the three of us had been hanging out. It was a relaxing evening. Then Abraham must have started in on Selena about something or somebody in our lives, the way he often did.

Things started quietly, as a discussion—I could hear them talking in the kitchen because the apartment was such an open space—but rapidly escalated into another full-blown argument. If Selena made up her mind about something, it was very hard to get her to change it. And, once Abraham didn't like something, he would do everything in his power to try to force people to do things his way, so interactions between them could get pretty intense. Often it really scared me when they started arguing.

"You can't always tell me what to do!" Selena cried, and that's when I decided that I needed to intervene.

I went into the kitchen and saw that Selena had lost it. She was trying to talk, but she was crying so hard that she couldn't take a breath. "What's going on here?" I asked, looking from Selena to her father.

Abraham turned and looked at me. "What are you doing to her?" he shouted.

"What are you talking about? This is all you, right here," I said.

Selena sank down to the floor and folded into herself, still sobbing. I went over to her and held her, putting her head on my chest and rocking her as if she were a small child as Abraham left and shut the door behind him.

Abraham and I continued to have these uncomfortable power struggles. Most of the tension between us was the result of incidents where I had to run interference and support Selena when she and her father were butting heads. Luckily, despite the fact that Abraham had tried in every way conceivable to keep us apart, once we were married, Abraham was old-school enough to honor me as Selena's husband. I think that he genuinely respected me, too, because I generally spoke my mind but was polite while doing it. I kept thinking that, as time went on, Abraham would learn to pick his battles, but that wasn't really in his nature. It wasn't in Selena's, either.

Once, for instance, the three of us—Abraham, Selena, and myself—went to the Hard Rock Cafe's grand opening in San Antonio. Selena was having a great time—she even went up and sang a song with the band Cheap Trick. After a while, though, Abraham was tired and wanted to leave.

"I'm ready to go now," he announced to Selena. "Enough fun. It's getting late."

"I don't want to leave yet," she said, and went off to find me. "My dad keeps telling me he wants to leave. Are you okay with it if we stay a little longer?"

"Yeah, I'm cool," I said.

"Good," Selena said, and went back to the stage.

Within minutes, Abraham had sought me out in the crowd and was standing in front of me, shaking his finger in that way he had. "You need to tell Selena that it's time to go," he said.

Of course, Abraham had always been the absolute authority in his family, so he believed that I must hold the same status in mine. He still didn't understand the egalitarian nature of my marriage with Selena.

"I'm sorry, Abraham," I said. "She doesn't want to go yet. We're going to stay."

He just shook his head in disgust and stalked off.

Another time, we were all eating in a restaurant after a show when a fan approached the table. I was sitting at one end with Selena. Most of the band members were present with their girlfriends or wives; Abraham was seated at the far end of the table.

The fan suddenly tossed a piece of paper between Selena and me. "Sign this!" the woman demanded.

Selena spun around. "I'm sorry, can you please wait until we're done eating?" she said. "Then I'll be happy to sign it." She turned her back on the woman and the fan left us, fuming under her breath.

This angered Abraham. "Why did you have to be so rude to that woman?" he demanded.

"She was rude first!" Selena said, equally infuriated. "How is it that somebody can just come up while I'm eating and toss something at me and you think that's perfectly okay?"

The argument continued to rage between them all through dinner, and even after we were back on the bus. Finally, I had no choice but to intervene.

"Look, man," I told Abraham. "Selena has every right to have a little peace and quiet to eat her dinner, just like the rest of us. There have to be some boundaries or she's going to burn out."

Abraham backed down, then, in a way he never would have done if it had been Selena telling him the same thing.

Despite these family quarrels, Selena and I were happier than we had ever been. I would come home from running errands and often find Selena cleaning or cooking. She loved playing her new role as wife. She was good at it, too. She even learned how to make a recipe for black-tipped shark that immediately became my favorite meal ever. I still don't know what ingredients she used to marinate that shark, but it was better than anything I'd ever tasted.

When we weren't on the road, Selena and I reveled in each other and in our new life. On some weekends, we went to San Antonio to visit my family and friends. Selena fit in right away with my parents, my grandparents, my aunts and uncles. She might have even been a little more outgoing with my family than with her own. Nobody saw her as a superstar, because she wasn't, not yet. Selena also had this thing about her that made people feel comfortable, no matter how famous she got—that was true from the first day I met her, and it was true until the day she died.

My family saw Selena as a normal, happily married young woman who loved to hang out in the backyard for a barbecue, toss a football, or lounge in a tire swing hanging from a tree. Then she'd get all dressed up and we'd go to a club, where she'd get onstage and have all of these people tripping out on that same person. It never failed to amaze me how Selena could cross between those two worlds without missing a beat.

Selena really knew how to have a good time, too. I remember showing up at my cousin Kenny's house in San Antonio one time, and walking in with Selena just as my cousins were mixing drinks that looked like creamy orange juice.

"What is that stuff?" I asked.

"Oh, you don't want any of this, this is for big boys only," Kenny said, waving his glass high in the air.

"What's it called?" Selena asked.

"A Salty Dog," Kenny's wife said.

Selena and I looked at each other and burst out laughing. "Let me try it," I said.

"I want to try it, too!" Selena insisted.

After a couple of Salty Dogs, Selena was the life of the party, sitting on the edge of Kenny's sofa and telling jokes with a bucket on top of her head. I don't know what she was doing, but she was being a goofball and making everybody laugh.

Because Selena was a Jehovah's Witness, she had never celebrated Christmas. Truthfully, I seldom did, either, because the band usually played on holidays. The first year we were married, however, the band was free on Christmas, and I took Selena home to my mom's house for the holiday.

My family had all bought Selena Christmas gifts, even though I'd told them that she didn't observe the holiday. Out of respect for Selena, they piled the gifts in my mom's room instead of putting them under the Christmas tree.

When I took Selena in there, she was floored. My family does it up big on Christmas. The bed was covered with brightly wrapped presents, all for her. Selena had never been part of a family Christmas celebration before and she loved it. Her religion was a serious subject to her, and a private one, too—one of the few subjects Selena never felt comfortable talking about to the media. That day she went wild, though, just ripping into those presents and enjoying herself like any excited little kid on Christmas. It was a joy for me to watch her.

Whenever Selena and I weren't visiting friends and family, we loved staying home to cook, putter, and watch TV. We fully enjoyed experiencing what we'd never had before: an open, loving relationship that we could share with the world, even holding hands on the street if we felt like it. Our love felt fresh again because we no longer had to tiptoe around and hide how we felt about each other.

It seemed that, despite Abraham flinging every possible obstacle in our path, we might be able to live happily ever after, even without Selena's fairy-tale wedding.

NINE

A HOUSE OF OUR OWN (SORT OF)
AND OUR PRACTICE FAMILY

Courtesy of Carmen M. Cadena

"That winter was so cold in Lake Jackson that my baby pigs died," Selena said. "But my mom brought them back to life."

I laughed. "You're not serious."

Selena was telling me this story as we walked around a mall in San Antonio. We were headed for her favorite store—the pet store—and she was telling me about having a pet chicken and pet piglets as a little kid. I loved her stories, because I'd never had a pet as a child.

"She did, really!" Selena said. "The pigs were dead and I was crying, so my mom decided to bring the pigs into the kitchen. We turned the oven on low and laid the piglets out on the oven door."

"That couldn't possibly work," I said, taking delight in my wife's brown eyes, which were dancing at the memory of her mother's heroics.

Selena grew solemn all of a sudden. "Those piggies warmed right up and walked again," she promised, and then started giggling.

Selena was an animal lover, and so was I. Maybe that's why, as soon as we had a house of our own, we started our practice family.

Or maybe it was just because Selena loved to buy things on impulse.

The house had been the subject of many late-night debates between us. Around the time Selena's lease on her apartment was due to be renewed, Abraham announced that he was making an offer on a house in his neighborhood—a house on Bloomington Street with a yard that connected to his own. A.B. already lived next door to Abraham, on the other side; if we moved in, the entire Quintanilla family would live in three adjoining houses.

"Uh-uh. No way am I going to live next to my father," Selena announced.

I had some doubts about living that close to Abraham, too, given his strong will and his temper. At the same time, I respected the man as both a manager and Selena's father, and I didn't usually feel like he could railroad me; we had developed a mutual respect, and occasionally Abraham called me "son."

By now, I had a better understanding of the Quintanilla family's dynamics. I knew how vitally important family was to them. Selena and her family members could really make each other angry to the nth degree, but eventually their disagreements usually blew over and things would be fine. They had worked hard to build their lives together. I didn't want to just come in and say, *Okay, we're married, now we're going to get as far away as we can.* That wasn't my style. I wasn't afraid of getting lost or railroaded if we lived next to Abraham. I had a strong sense of self even at that age.

Plus, there was a certain logic to us all living nearby, since we spent so many hours working together on music. Not only that, Abraham was generously going to buy the house himself and let Selena and me live in it rent-free.

"If we do this, we could save up for a house," I pointed out to her. "And we see your family all the time on the road anyway. What's the difference?"

"The difference is that they'd be right next door," Selena argued. "If we had friends come over or any kind of get-together, you know my dad is going to want to be there."

"Well, we'd probably invite him anyway," I said. "We usually do. Look, I'm cool with the idea. You know that I'm fine with being around your family. You decide. Either way is fine with me. We can always live in San Antonio if you want more distance."

My family and friends were all in San Antonio, but Selena's family was all in Corpus. In the end, she decided that it made sense to accept her father's offer. "That way we can take our time and maybe even build a house we really like," she said.

So, within three months of being married, Selena and I had our own house. After painting it, tearing up the carpets, and putting in new floors, Selena and I went to a furniture store in Corpus to buy a few things. That's when she spotted a headboard that was also a huge aquarium and declared that she had to have it. It was Plexiglas, eighteen inches high, with a black border all around it.

"It's completely art deco," Selena said. "It'll be perfect with our black carpet and black sofa."

I was doubtful. "It doesn't even have a filter," I said. "I'd have to build a filtration system into it. And if you want a saltwater aquarium, well, that's a lot of maintenance."

"Come on, please?" Selena said. "It would look really cool in our bedroom."

I couldn't ever say no to her when Selena turned her big brown eyes on me and made that sad puppy face. I started buying books on saltwater aquariums and figuring out how to build the filtration system. It was a lot of work, but eventually I managed to slit the aquarium in a way that allowed me to insert a PVC pipe into it and mount it to a pump. For a while we had a beautiful aquarium with no fish in it at all, because I had to keep adjusting the filter and making sure the water stayed clear and had the right levels of salt.

Meanwhile, Selena was poring through books on saltwater fish and exclaiming over their colors and shapes. They weren't cheap fish, and I knew that keeping them healthy would be a big job. But we were both really excited when the day finally came that we could add fish. And the aquarium was, as Selena had predicted, the perfect addition to our bedroom, a moving work of art.

But why stop there? With Selena, more was often better. One day, I came home and she said, "Look what I bought!"

It was another aquarium. This one was octagonal and taller than I was. It had a black base about a foot tall, and another black piece with a clock set into it. Luckily, this aquarium came with all of the necessary filtration equipment, but I still had to put it together. It was worth it, though, because Selena loved those fish so much.

Now, as we walked to the pet store, Selena spotted a pen full of puppies outside the door. Immediately she ran over to it and put her fingers in, letting the dogs lick her and nip at her fingers. She was nearly bouncing up and down with delight, making me smile as I watched her.

They were cute puppies, to be sure: fuzzy, lively little Pomeranians tumbling all over each other in their nest of newspaper shavings. Most were tan and white. They were sweet looking, but Selena was captivated by the only black puppy in the litter. "Look at this one!" she squealed. "Doesn't she look just like a little bear? I really want her!"

What would we do with a dog while we were on the road? Still, I could never deny Selena anything. "Let's check her out," I suggested.

There was a room in the back where customers could sit and play with dogs they were considering buying. A store clerk led us back there and talked to us about the pros and cons of Pomeranians as pets, and the particulars about this puppy's birth date and vaccinations. She might as well have been singing opera. Neither of us was listening. Selena was down on the floor, rolling around with the dog, and I knew the deal was done.

We acted like parents with a newborn, buying every possible accessory for that puppy. We named her Pebbles and took her on the road with us until she was old enough to stay home with our housekeeper whenever we were gone.

Pebbles became queen of our house. She also started our dog collection.

A few months after getting her, my friend Jesse came to Corpus to visit. He and I went shopping at another mall and happened to walk past a pet store. I glanced in the window and spotted four Siberian husky puppies. One of them had incredible markings on his face, including a black cross straight up and down his nose and across his eyes.

"That's a cool-looking dog," I said, reaching down to pat him.

"Why don't you get him?" Jesse asked.

"I'll think about it," I said, but I wasn't serious.

When I got home later, I started showing Selena the clothes I'd bought at the mall.

"Did you see anything else you liked there?" she asked.

"Hey, tell her about the dog," Jesse said.

"Oh, yeah, we saw a cute husky puppy. Really cool looking," I told her, and described the dog's markings.

Right away, Selena said, "Let's go see him. Can we go back there and see him?"

I laughed because she was so excited. "Another dog? Pebbles would kill us."

"Come on," she pleaded. "I really want to see that puppy. Let's go back there and check him out."

Oh, man, here we go, I thought, but I drove us all back to the pet store anyway. I gave Selena a little speech on the way there. "We're just going to look at the puppies," I reminded her. "We've already got Pebbles. Now don't freak out and all of a sudden want to buy him. Don't get carried away."

"Okay," she said. "I promise."

As soon as we got to the pet store, though, Selena went crazy. "Which one is it? Is that him right there?"

She ran over to the cage and picked up the puppy with the black face markings, holding him close. "Oh my God, I love him. Let's bring him home. Can we?"

"Are you sure?" I asked.

"You all are going to get him for real?" Jesse asked, amazed by Selena's excitement. He was laughing, too, because he'd started this whole thing.

"Of course we are," Selena said, and off we went with our new dog. We named him "Jax" for my Jackson guitar.

Jax turned out to be a really cool dog. Everybody in the neighborhood was scared of him, though, because he had weird, bright blue eyes that almost looked like marbles and those black markings on his face. Our house was near an elementary school, and I remember one time being out in the yard when this kid came along and started banging on the fence, trying to tease the dog. I could just see the kid's face in the cracks between the fence slats, and his little hands up on top of it. I knew what he was going to do before he did it.

Jax knew, too. He sat and waited for the little boy to reach up, grab the top of the fence, and pull himself up to see over it. Then Jax jumped straight up and popped the boy in the forehead with his nose, so that the kid took off running.

Only Pebbles, our Pomeranian, told Jax what to do. She remained the queen despite the fact that Jax was three times her size. Whenever we let her out in the yard, Pebbles would run up to Jax and tug on his ears with her teeth. She was a rowdy little thing.

Our dog party didn't stop there. One day, Selena was outside cutting the grass—she loved doing that—when a woman walked by with two gigantic beasts. When I came home from running errands, I turned the corner in the car and saw Selena standing there talking to the woman with these humongous dogs the size of ponies.

"What the hell are those?" I muttered.

The minute I parked in the driveway and got out of the car, Selena said, "Babe, come over here. Meet our neighbor Margie and her great dogs."

One of the dogs, Max, was about the scariest-looking creature I'd ever seen, a brindle dog with a huge head and jaws that looked like they could crush a truck. As I approached Selena and Margie, that dog opened his mouth, looked right at me, and let out a bark from hell. I swear that the ground shook when Selena walked him over to meet me.

Selena started telling me about Max and the other dog, a female named Brandy, informing me that they were English bull mastiffs. She lectured me on the origin of the breed, what they were like as pets and on and on, as though she hadn't just seen them for the first time herself. As she talked, I stared at her, thinking, *Oh, no, do not even think what I know you're thinking, Selena. No way can we handle dogs like these.*

After a few minutes, I went inside to unload the groceries, making the mistake of leaving Selena out there with those dogs. Little did I know that Brandy was pregnant, much less that Selena would tell Margie that she wanted one of the puppies.

Later, I found out from Margie that she'd tried to convince Selena to ask my permission to bring home a bull mastiff, but Selena had said, "Oh, don't you worry about Chris. He'll come around."

A few months later, she surprised me with the puppy, which was already half Selena's size even though it was just a couple of months old. I looked at Selena and said, "You bought it, didn't you?"

She ignored my question. "Oh, Chris, look how cute she is!"

"That dog's going to be bigger than you are," I warned, but I could feel myself weakening. The puppy was cute and Selena's enthusiasm was as contagious as her laugh. Plus, it always melted my heart to see her with baby animals, because it was so easy to imagine how it would be one day with children of our own. I had no doubt that Selena would be as amazing at motherhood as she was at everything else.

Selena set the dog down on the ground and we both smiled like proud parents as we watched the puppy leap around. English bull mastiffs are such big dogs that their legs are kind of stiff and they're extremely clumsy in their early months. It was like watching a colt in our yard. Now I was in love with this puppy, too. I knew it would be an awesome dog.

"Okay," I said. "Let's keep her."

We named that puppy Taylor. What I didn't know—how many times will I have to confess this?—was that, when Selena went to Margie's house, she bought not just Taylor, but another puppy, too. She was afraid to tell me, though, so she had Margie hold the other dog.

"She wanted to break the news to you slowly," Margie told me later.

At the time, all Selena said to me was, "Gosh, I feel so bad for Margie. She can't find a home for that last puppy."

Still clueless, I said, "Oh, I'm sure somebody will happen along who wants to buy a dog."

Selena kept mentioning how much trouble Margie was having selling that last puppy, though, and at last some red flags went up. I knew Selena well enough to realize that she had probably already bought the damn thing.

I came to grips with the idea pretty quickly. What was one more pet? But I didn't make it easy for Selena. In fact, I did whatever I could to make it harder. Whenever she brought up the subject of the last puppy, I'd just say, "Oh, that's too bad it's difficult for Margie. I wish we could help her out, but we've already got three dogs, and those mastiffs grow up to be so big."

Finally, one day Selena just came out with the truth. "I did it. I bought the last puppy. It's ours, Chris."

I grinned. "I already figured that out."

She whacked my arm. "You did? You already knew, and you just let me keep on talking and talking? You didn't say anything?"

"Hey, a guy's got to have his fun around here," I said.

Selena went off and called Margie, who brought the last puppy over to our house. We named that dog Winnie.

As Margie got out of the car with the dog, she said, "Please don't be mad at me, Chris."

"Dude, I know how Selena is," I said. "She doesn't need any coaxing. She just loves animals that much."

And it really was fine in the end. Selena and I both loved going out in the yard to wrestle with Winnie and Taylor. They'd jump and drool all over us. They loved to chase us, too, always trying to trip us the way lions trip their prey, by nipping at our heels. Sometimes I took Winnie and Taylor over to the schoolyard on weekends, too, where I'd run with them in a wide-open field, or Selena would walk them around the neighborhood and encourage the kids to come and pat them.

Selena loved playing with all of the neighborhood kids, but there was one in particular she developed a special affection for, a young boy with a squeaky voice named Tim. Tim loved basketball more than anything in the world, and he was a big fan of Michael Jordan.

One day, as we stood around in the yard playing with the dogs and joking with Tim, he announced with something like despair in his voice that he wanted a pair of basketball shoes called Air Jordans.

"My mom's not going to buy them for me, though," he said with a sigh.

"Why not?" Selena asked.

"Too much money," Tim said. "And if I wait to save up for those sneakers, they're going to be sold out."

"Tell you what," Selena said. "I'll go get you the shoes, and in exchange, you can help me wash the cars and do things around the yard for a few weeks. Deal?"

She took him to buy the shoes, and you never saw a happier boy than Tim.

You would think that four dogs would be enough for anyone, but one more was about to join our practice family. The band was playing in Houston, and after our sound check for the show, we all went over to the Galleria Mall. Selena and I went our own way there and agreed to meet the band later.

As we were walking around, we passed a pet store and stepped inside "just to look," as Selena always said—a dangerous proposition, coming from her. There we saw a little firecracker of a miniature Doberman. He was tiny but feisty, really trying to kill this little toy in his pen, shaking it back and forth in his mouth until Selena was laughing so hard that tears streamed down her face.

"I just love him!" she said. "Look at him, Chris!"

"Oh, no," I said, but I was laughing, too. "That is a pretty cool dog," I admitted. "If you want to look at him, let's go."

In we went. Selena was wearing a long, sheer dress with gauze under layers that went all the way down to her ankles. We carried the puppy into the back room, and that little Doberman was flopping all around in Selena's arms because he was so excited.

Finally Selena set him down on the floor and the puppy started zipping around our legs. It didn't take him long before he was playfully nipping at her dress with his sharp little teeth, shaking it from side to side.

Selena didn't care. She was cracking up. "Look at him, he's crazy," she said.

That dog *was* crazy, too. Every time I put my hand down to pat him, he had to have his nose on my fingers. "I think I'm in love," I said.

"Me, too," Selena said. "Let's get him."

We bought the puppy and immediately decided to name him André, after André the Giant. As we were heading back to the bus, I suddenly remembered Abraham. "Oh, no," I said. "What's your dad going to say about us bringing a puppy on board the bus?"

"Don't worry. I'll tell him," Selena said.

I fully expected Abraham to jump down my throat and say something along the lines of, "Son, what's wrong with you? You already have all these dogs. Why do you need another one?"

But, to my amazement, Abraham was an even easier mark than Selena. As soon as she said, "Hey, look what we got," he went nuts and started talking baby talk to our little dog.

I handed André to Abraham, and you never saw a happier man. The puppy licked his face and Abraham laughed.

They were terrific dogs, and Selena and I were happy playing house and practicing our parenting skills on our furry pack.

It was Selena's idea to get a dog, but it was my idea to own a pet snake. I had always wanted one, I told Selena one day.

"You want a what?" she asked, incredulous. "But why? You can't call a snake to come over and sit next to you, and it'll never lick your cheek or play with you."

"I don't know," I admitted. "I just think snakes are really cool."

Selena was always a good sport. As I started bringing books home about pet snakes, learning which ones were better than others and how to maintain them, she read the books right along with me and learned as well. Finally, we settled on a ball python, because they were docile snakes that would typically roll themselves into a ball if they were threatened instead of trying to bite. Another plus was that they didn't grow any bigger than five feet long.

We found a pet store that specialized in exotic pets. They stocked all different kinds of snakes and lizards. I could tell by the way her eyes skittered around to every corner of the store that Selena was trying to pull off acting brave, but feeling jumpy inside.

"It's okay," I reminded her. "They're all in cages and aquariums."

When one of the clerks approached us, I told him that we were thinking about getting a snake. He and I started discussing pythons. To my amazement, Selena just stood next to me without saying a word—a rare occasion.

I had already acquired a forty-gallon aquarium tank, a heat lamp, heat rocks, and everything else that we needed. When I told the clerk this, he went into the back room and returned with a ball python wrapped around his arm. As soon as Selena saw that, she was gone. She didn't just walk fast. She ran out the door, then turned around and stared at me from outside the store, big-eyed.

I started cracking up. "It's okay," I said, and then she started laughing, too. "Come on," I encouraged her.

She came back into the store slowly, keeping her eye on that python, which by now had wrapped itself around my arm. The clerk told me all about the snake and its feeding habits—it ate live mice—while Selena stepped a little closer.

Once she looked calmer, I said, "Come on. Check him out." I held the snake toward her on my arm.

Selena put her arm out. The python went right over to it and wrapped itself around her arm. She tensed for a minute, then relaxed again.

We brought the snake home in a little sack, kind of like a pillowcase, and put it in our aquarium. Selena was nervous around the snake for a while, but after about a month had passed, she relaxed.

Ball pythons are binge feeders; they'll eat, then go for long periods of time without being hungry again. A couple of weeks after buying the python, I decided that it had probably had enough time to adjust to its new environment. It was time to buy a mouse and try feeding it.

I went out to the pet store and came home with a white mouse that had little brown spots on it. I had only bought a single mouse, not wanting to have one left over if the snake wasn't hungry enough to eat two. "You want to watch the snake eat?" I asked Selena.

"Yeah, I want to see it," she said, which sort of surprised me.

I dropped the mouse into the snake's cage and we both watched. Nothing happened. Finally we decided to leave the snake alone and turn out the lights.

The next morning, the mouse was still alive. It was in the aquarium drinking the snake's water and having a grand time scampering around inside that forty-gallon tank, using the snake as a playground.

"We can't just leave that poor mouse in there, feeling scared all of the time that the snake will eat it," Selena said. "Let's go back to the pet store and get him a little cage."

The next thing that happened, of course, was that we started building a mouse habitat, attaching all of these plastic cages and tubes for the mouse to live in, until we pretty much had a mouse mansion. Selena named him "Bugsy" because of his big eyes, and talked to him all the time.

One night, Selena was getting ready to go out with Suzette. I was watching television while she showered and did her hair and makeup. I don't know why, but suddenly I decided that it must be time to try to feed the snake again.

I got up and took the mouse out of its cage, then dropped it into the snake's aquarium. Nothing happened, so I turned off the light and left the room.

A few minutes later, I decided to check on Bugsy again. I snapped on the light, thinking I'd take the little mouse out of the aquarium and return it to its cage. Instead, I found the snake chowing down; its head was up and just Bugsy's back feet and tail were sticking out of the python's mouth.

I started tripping, knowing how upset Selena would be. "Well," I said to the snake, shaking my head. "You got him. He's all yours." I snapped off the light and shut the door again, hoping Selena wouldn't want to check on Bugsy before she left.

"All right, I'm ready to go," Selena said a few minutes later.

I walked her to the door and kissed her good-bye. "Love you. Have a good time."

As soon as she was gone, I ran into the room with the aquarium and turned the light back on. Sure enough, the snake was done: he had a big ball going down his throat.

"Please hurry up and get rid of that," I told him. "You've only got a couple of hours before she gets back, dude."

Selena went straight to bed that night, and I couldn't bring myself to tell her about Bugsy. Instead, I lied. In the morning, I said, "Hey, I think Bugsy got out of his cage."

"What, really?" she asked.

"Yeah, well, he's not in his cage anymore," I said. I just didn't have the heart to tell her.

Selena grew increasingly comfortable having the python in the house, and even watched me feed it mice from time to time. She had no trouble showing the snake to friends and telling them everything she knew about pythons. She'd act like the queen of snakes sometimes, even sticking her hand in the aquarium to touch the snake's muscled back like she had no problem at all with reptiles.

One time, however, we went out on tour and came back to find the snake gone. Usually we'd get dropped off by the bus early in the morning after a show the night before. I'd wake Selena and she would just sit up, walk out of the bus, and go straight to bed, where she'd pull the covers up and go right back to sleep.

Meanwhile, I would check the house, turning the lights on in each room to look around and make sure everything was okay. When I reached the room where we kept the snake, I realized that all was not as I'd left it. We always kept that door shut on the off chance the python escaped, but the door was wide-open.

"Shoot," I said, and went straight to the aquarium. Sure enough, it was empty.

I looked all over for the snake. Finally I went into the bedroom and said, "Hey, Selena?" I shook her shoulder a little to wake her. "I'm going to tell you something, but don't freak out."

"What?" she mumbled.

"The snake isn't in the aquarium."

She sat right up. "What?"

I repeated it. "I looked everywhere."

Selena climbed out of bed and we started combing through the house. She was a little jumpy now, because we didn't know where that snake might pop out from; even though it was almost four feet long, I knew the python could fit in a pretty small hole.

A few days went by. Finally, one morning I was outside with the dogs when all of a sudden I heard Selena screaming my name hysterically. "Chris! Chris, get in here!"

I ran inside and found Selena standing on top of the bed, jumping up and down and yelling. We had a king-size mattress; beneath it were two box springs pushed together.

"What the hell is going on?" I asked, panting.

Then I saw it: the snake's head was poking out from between those two box springs. That poor python looked just as terrified as Selena, and I started laughing.

"It's not funny!" Selena said.

"It's okay, I got him," I said. "You're fine."

Nothing I said could coax Selena off that bed. Finally I separated the mattresses enough to reach in and pull the snake out, talking gently to it the whole time, knowing that the poor thing probably couldn't even hear me over my wife's screams.

Finally, when Selena calmed down and the snake was safely stowed in its aquarium, I said, "I thought you weren't afraid of snakes. Or was that all just big talk?"

"Shut up," she said. "You know how I am."

"I do," I said, and kissed her.

TEN

A WILD RIDE WITH SELENA

Courtesy of Ernest "Choco" Garza

The front door slammed so hard that the walls shook. I had been playing guitar, trying to work something out. Now I looked up. "Selena?" I called.

She stormed into the house but walked right past me without saying a word, her face dark with anger, her hair flying, muttering something I couldn't quite catch.

"Selena?" I followed her into the bedroom, where I found her just sitting there, her hands balled into fists, tears streaming down her face. "What is it? What's wrong?"

"We have to move," she announced. "I don't want to be here anymore. I can't stay in this house!"

"Why not?"

"It's my dad," Selena said miserably. "We need our own space, Chris. We need to be on our own. Really on our own!"

I knew what she meant. We had been living in the house next door to Selena's parents for almost a year, and we often felt like we were being watched. The entire Quintanilla family was still living in the same modest Corpus Christi neighborhood; Abraham and Marcella in one house, A.B. with his wife and kids in another; and

Selena and me in the third. Now it looked like Selena had gotten into another argument with Abraham. Most likely it had been about the boutique that she wanted to open.

Whenever Selena tried to discuss her desire to get into the fashion business, Abraham's standard response was to try to talk her out of it. "What do you want to do that for?" he'd say. "That's a crazy idea. You're making plenty of money and you don't have enough time as it is. Why don't you just sit back and enjoy life?"

I could see Abraham's point. It was true that the band was making considerably more money now than we ever had before. Selena and I were comfortable financially. I earned a good salary as a guitarist under the umbrella of Los Dinos, and Selena and her family were commanding more money than ever for live shows.

While some people accused Abraham of controlling Selena and her money, that simply wasn't true. Whatever Selena and the band earned, Abraham would first take care of the payroll. Then the family split whatever was left in four equal parts. They divided the money from the Coca-Cola sponsorship as well, with the family splitting the first three payments in a year three ways and Selena keeping the fourth.

Opening fashion boutiques probably wouldn't add much to Selena's income, at least not at first, and getting this kind of business up and running would be extremely time-consuming. On the other hand, living with Selena had shown me firsthand that she was an incredibly hard worker, and I knew how much she wanted to do this. Her family didn't fully grasp how badly Selena needed to do something just for herself.

The longer I knew and loved Selena, the clearer it became that she loved me in part because I accepted her completely. No matter what she wanted to try—whether it was something as small as wanting that aquarium headboard or a new dog, or a plan as complex as starting a fashion business on top of her musical career—I loved Selena for who she was, and never put up the kind of resistance she often felt from her family and even from certain friends.

Selena was creative and she could be exceedingly impulsive, but no matter what ideas she expressed to me, I was never negative—I'd had enough negativity in my own family when I first tried to become a rock guitarist, so I knew how bad that could feel. Instead, she and I would talk things through in an attempt to encourage Selena to be less impulsive, do a little planning, and articulate her vision clearly enough so that she could see whether her idea was workable or not. Her dreams were my dreams. If something was important to Selena, it was important to me, too. That's how much I loved her.

Selena was quick to appreciate this about me, too. "Thank you, Chris," she'd say, whenever I supported her position on something. "Thank you for helping me."

Now, Selena brought the newspaper into the kitchen, where I watched her comb through the classified ads and circle various houses for rent.

"You really want to move this time?" I asked. We had been down this road together before, usually after similar family arguments.

"Oh, I really do," Selena said. "We need to get out of here."

Without much more discussion, we got in the car and started driving around, even pulling into the driveways of houses at the addresses she'd circled. Afterward, Selena made some phone calls, but that was the end of it. I'm sure part of the reason she dropped the idea was that it would be a lot of work to move, and she was

usually exhausted just from her recording and performance obligations. But Selena wasn't ready yet to put even that much distance
between herself and her family.

To me, it didn't really matter where we lived. What mattered to
me was Selena's happiness. As long as she wanted to live in that
neighborhood, and in that house alongside her father and brother,
I could be happy there. If Selena ever really wanted to leave, I would
be right beside her, helping her every step of the way.

Selena was as supportive of me as I was of her, with one important
exception: the time I talked about leaving Los Dinos to pursue my
dream of starting a rock band, she shut me down cold.

We were nearly at the pinnacle of our success by 1993, and I
loved making a living playing in a Tejano band as successful as Los
Dinos. That was my work and I took pride in it. I even developed a
certain love and respect for Tejano music. Still, I was a musician
before I met Selena, and I had my own taste. I continued to listen
to rock music and even introduced Selena to a lot of the bands I
liked. A big part of me still longed to play that music.

Selena and I always listened to music on road trips, and she was
open-minded. She could appreciate most of my choices, which included everything from Alice in Chains and Pearl Jam to Green Day.
We had a sort of unspoken agreement that she would listen to my
music if I listened to hers; at the time, her favorite artists were Bon-
nie Raitt, Whitney Houston, and Janet Jackson. Selena especially
loved Jackson's song "Black Cat," which Janet wrote for her *Rhythm
Nation 1814* album. I can't even count how many times Selena and
I listened to that single.

After we had been married for a few months, I confessed to Selena that I still harbored those desires to play a different kind of music. I had become a fan of Latin rock, and I was listening to a lot of that on my headphones or with her. I thought maybe I could start a Latin rock band and make my own way in that direction.

"I love Tejano music," I told Selena, "and you know I love playing with Los Dinos. But you have to admit that Tejano music isn't really geared toward guitar players. I'm just playing the same chords over and over again."

"That's not true," she protested. "A.B. lets you play a lot of things the way you want."

She was right, but even though I was pushing the boundaries a little bit in the context of Tejano music, I still couldn't see any way to continue developing as a guitar player if I restricted myself to this genre. The music just wasn't challenging enough and I was feeling stifled, I told her.

"Uh-huh," Selena said. She was watching me with an odd sort of sideways look while I fumbled through this conversation.

I tried again. "I want to try something different," I said. "I love you, and I love being onstage with you. You know that. But I'm bored, Selena, and that's the truth. It's time I tried something else, like Latin rock."

Selena came around to stand in front of me. She looked me in the eye without saying anything at first. She just pinned me in place with her dark eyes.

"What?" I asked, suddenly nervous.

"That's not going to happen," Selena said. "If you quit the band and do something else, Chris, it will be over between us."

"What are you talking about?" I asked in alarm. By now my

palms were sweating because of that cold look she was giving me. "Why would it be over just because I wanted to try playing another kind of music?"

Her voice was still calm, but with an undercurrent of tension that made me afraid to touch her. "You would be on the road away from me," she said. "I've been on the road all my life, so I know what it's like for guys. I saw how you were with women and drinking before we were together. If you and I were on the road separately, I would think about that and worry."

As soon as Selena said that, I knew that it was the truth. Even though I was a year older, Selena had been on the road far longer than I had; she had been doing this since she was a kid. She knew the reality of the music business.

We didn't know life apart from each other as a couple. Since falling in love, we had always been together—on buses, in planes, and on stages at this hotel or that arena. Selena knew that, no matter how much we vowed to be faithful to one another, that vow would be too easy to break if we weren't playing in a band together.

Selena had also seen me at my worst. She had known me when I got arrested for drunk driving, and she had nearly left me when I trashed that hotel room with the road crew and nearly trashed her family's reputation in the process.

My wife had taught me that the meaning of true love is forgiveness. Here was somebody who had seen me make some of the worst mistakes of my life, yet she had accepted my apologies and believed in me. I owed Selena the same kind of trust and loyalty that she had shown me.

"Yeah," I said. "I guess you're right."

Selena and Abraham. / Selena y Abraham.

Selena at age thirteen. / Selena a los trece años de edad.

Selena at age thirteen. / Selena a los trece años de edad.

Selena poses. / Selena posando.

For Selena, the show must go on. No one had any inkling that she was under the weather. / Para Selena, el espectáculo debe continuar y nadie tiene idea de que no se siente bien.

Selena hams it up on the side of the highway. / Selena posa exageradamente al lado de la autopista.

Selena on the phone before one of the shows. / Selena al teléfono antes de uno de sus conciertos.

Selena in great spirits. / Selena de muy buen humor.

Selena dancing and singing at a performance. / Selena bailando y cantando en un concierto.

Selena accepts an award. / Selena acepta un premio.

Taken at one of her many photo shoots. / Selena en una de sus muchas sesiones fotográficas.

A great picture from one of her many photo shoots. / Una fotografía excelente obtenida en una de sus muchas sesiones fotográficas.

Selena at the grand opening of the Selena Boutique & Salon, October 1994. / Selena en la inauguración de la tienda Selena Boutique & Salon, octubre de 1994.

Selena and I at the Selena Boutique & Salon, October 1994. / Selena y yo en Selena Boutique & Salon, octubre de 1994.

Selena backstage at a concert in San Antonio, December 1994. / Selena tras bastidores en un concierto en San Antonio, diciembre de 1994.

Selena performing at a concert in San Antonio, December 1994. / Selena cantando en un concierto en San Antonio, diciembre de 1994.

Selena performing with the Barrio Boys, December 1994. / Selena cantando con los Barrio Boys, diciembre de 1994.

Selena at one of her fashion shows, December 1994. / Selena en uno de sus desfiles de moda, diciembre de 1994.

With Selena in Vegas. / Con Selena, en Las Vegas.

Selena smiled, her brown eyes alight with warmth again. "So you'll stay with Los Dinos?"

"I'll keep backing you up," I said. I meant what I said to apply to our lives both offstage and on, and Selena knew it.

I never resented Selena for making me stay. Far from it. What possible gripe could I have? I was making a living playing my guitar. I was in a Tejano band, true, but it was a badass Tejano band fronted by the love of my life.

Most important of all, this girl had my back, and I was going to have hers until we were old and left this earth. Little did I know that my time with her would be so short.

I had been wanting a motorcycle for a while. My father was a motorcycle rider until he got into a massive accident. My cousins and uncles on my father's side always had bikes around, too. Finally I told Selena that I was going to buy one for myself.

Most women I know have problems accepting the idea that the thrill of riding a motorcycle is worth the risk, but not Selena. Right up there with loving her family, our dogs, fashion, and me, she was crazy about any kind of vehicle. She excitedly accompanied me to the dealer in San Antonio when I bought the bike I'd been longing for—a Kawasaki Ninja.

On the drive back home to Corpus Christi, Selena drew up beside me on the highway in her BMW M3. "Race you," she called, goading me into it with one of those wild looks in her eyes.

"You bet," I said.

Within seconds, we were flying side by side down the highway. The bike wouldn't break 100 mph no matter how flat I lay on that gas tank to decrease the wind resistance or how hard I pushed it. Selena easily pulled in front of me, laughing her foolish head off as she passed, then gunned the BMW even faster just to prove her point: she'd won another dare.

Selena and I spent as much of our time together as possible, even when we weren't on the road. Despite having been married a year and having known each other for three, we were still fully aware every day of how lucky we were to be married now, because we could do things like just go to the grocery store. Life couldn't get any better than that.

Selena especially loved going for rides on that motorcycle with me, especially at night when it wasn't so hot. We'd cruise along the shoreline in Corpus Christi, admiring all of the fancy houses on the waterfront. Sometimes we would pull over and park, then get off the bike to sit on the seawall or walk along the jetties, just as we had when we were seeing each other secretly.

Not long after I got the Ninja, Selena and I had taken just such a cooling night ride, her body pressed against mine as we leaned around the turns, the breeze in our faces. We were resting on the seawall, admiring the reflection of the lights on the water, when she suddenly declared, "I want to learn how to drive the bike."

"Um, how about no?" I said. "No way."

"Why not?" Selena started to argue with me.

Maybe it was because she grew up as the youngest in her family, or maybe it was because she was the most like Abraham. For whatever reason, Selena was one of the most stubborn people I've ever known. She never liked anyone to tell her "no"—not A.B., Suzette, or her parents, much less her own husband, whom she knew she had wrapped around her little finger.

"Oh, come on, Chris. I can drive a motorcycle if you can do it," she said.

"You think it's easy to drive this motorcycle?" I asked in disbelief. "It's not like riding a bicycle, you know. You just think the Ninja is lightweight because it's always upright when you get on it. But I can promise you this: if you drove this motorcycle and let it lean past a certain point, it would fall over and you wouldn't be able to pick it back up. It would probably fall on your leg and break it."

Now Selena was giving me that puppy look with her big brown eyes and frowning. "But I want to learn how to drive the bike," she insisted.

I sighed. I knew Selena well enough by now to understand that, once she got an idea in her head about something she wanted to do, there was no stopping her. Selena was like our mini Doberman, André, with a toy. She would shake that idea of hers until she'd succeeded in tearing it to pieces, and God help anybody who tried to take it away.

"Okay," I said at last. "We'll go to the grocery store parking lot to see if you can balance on the bike. But that's all we're going to do, okay?"

"Okay," she promised.

Selena was fairly mechanical and a very hands-on person. She also loved to drive, so it wasn't really any surprise to me that, within minutes of me explaining them, she understood how the clutch, the brake, and the gears worked on the motorcycle. This, plus the fact that we were now in a huge, empty parking lot, put me a little more at ease.

"Okay, I'm getting on behind you," I said. "I'll hold the bike up."

She straddled the bike in front of me. "This is so cool," she said.

Cool unless you wreck my bike, I thought. "Yeah, it is cool, as long as you're careful," I reminded her. "Just think what your dad will do to me if I let you get hurt. All right. I'm getting off now. See if you can keep the bike balanced."

Selena wobbled a little from side to side. "Whoa! You're right. It is heavy."

"Remember that," I warned. "You're really going to get hurt if you start to fall over and don't put your foot down in time to catch yourself."

I showed her how to work the clutch and throttle, telling her to imagine her hand on the bar was like her foot working the accelerator. We talked things through as she engaged the clutch and explored the brakes. Meanwhile, I was thinking, *Bad idea to do this, Chris.*

But there was no backing out now. Selena's dark eyes were bright with excitement beneath the big helmet. Just then, the bike did a little hiccup, and she jumped. "What's that?" she asked, looking down at the motorcycle between her knees.

"It's cool," I said. "You're in first gear now."

"Can I ride it? For real?"

I had to smile. "Sure. Go for it. Click it up into second gear, but don't go past that. And remember where your brakes are!" I yelled as Selena started to drive away from me. "That's the most important thing!"

Selena took off slowly and without wobbling. I was proud of her; the bike didn't jump forward or stall. It was a nice, smooth start.

In seconds, of course, she was all the way across the parking lot and I couldn't see anything but the lights on my bike. "Okay!" I yelled. "That's far enough. You can come back now."

Selena rode back toward me, the big motorcycle purring between her knees. "How do I do the other gears?" she asked.

I taught her that, too, and then Selena took off around the parking lot again. She drove for about five minutes, getting more and more comfortable. Soon she started doing figure eights while I held my breath, watching her. As always, Selena had surprised me by how quickly she could learn something new.

She rode back eventually and said, "I think I got it."

"You do," I agreed. "You're doing everything right. Now let's try adding in the blinkers and practice that." I hadn't wanted to teach her too many things at once, but Selena had no trouble using the turn signals as she toured the parking lot again.

Pretty soon she was beside me again. "Get on," she suggested.

"Ha-ha. That's really funny," I said, rolling my eyes at her. "How about you get off."

"Come on, please?" Selena said. "Can I drive home?"

"You're scaring me," I said. "No. I can't let you do that. We have to get on the highway to drive home."

Selena, of course, got that bullheaded expression and started arguing. "What if I just stay on the access road?"

"That's even scarier," I said. "There are all kinds of intersections and stop signs."

"I'll go real slow," she promised. "Please?"

Eventually, she wore me down. *What's the harm?* I decided. If I were on the back of the bike, I could take control of the machine if she made a mistake.

"All right. Let's do it," I said.

Her grin was wide and white beneath that helmet as I got on the back of the bike behind her.

Selena eased the bike carefully out of the parking lot and onto the access road. As we got to the light near the access ramp for the highway, she wobbled a bit but I held us steady. That made me realize that she would probably do better on the highway; we'd be safer if she didn't have to stop or turn. Plus, there would be little traffic at night.

"Go ahead," I yelled over the engine. "Get on the highway."

"For real?"

I could hear the smile in her voice. "Yeah, get on the highway and see what's up."

Onto the highway we went. Selena started out at a gentle cruising speed, maybe 60 mph, but before too long she hit 65, then 70 mph.

"That's it! That's fast enough!" I yelled, tapping her side. I could hear her laughing through her helmet, but she slowed down a little.

Our ride was almost without incident. I started to relax. Selena was a good driver in a car and, despite her love of speed, she seemed fairly steady on a motorcycle.

The one thing that hadn't occurred to me until it was time to exit off the highway ramp was that Selena really hadn't had enough experience on a motorcycle to know how it would react. She had never made a turn off one street and onto another.

I was in a near panic. I lifted my visor and hurriedly started yelling things at her, telling Selena how to lean when she wanted to change lanes or turn a corner, demonstrating by pressing my body against hers.

When it was time to actually hit the exit ramp, Selena was still going too fast. "Slow down!" I yelled.

Thankfully, the light was green as we came off the highway.

Selena made the right turn successfully, cruising right through it. Then we had to make a quick left. Unfortunately, Selena decided to lean the bike before I did, so that the bike started turning before we reached the intersection.

I had to think fast. If I tried to fight her and the bike by leaning the other way, I risked having her straighten up, and that momentum could tip us over. If I sat up straight, she might lean even more and flip us over as well. It was going to be bad if I fought her in any way.

Finally I decided to lean with her, just a little. We popped a curb and went right over somebody's front yard, then came down hard off that curb and coasted onto the street. I felt Selena stiffen a little against me as she panicked. "Oh no!" she yelled.

"It's fine, it's fine. Don't panic. Just keep driving," I said, even though inside, I was yelling the same thing she was. The last thing I wanted to do was crash on our own street and have Abraham find out.

I told Selena to stop at the corner before we were close enough for her father to see us. "Why?" she yelled.

"What if your dad is outside for whatever reason, or he hears the motorcycle come up and decides to look out the window?" I yelled. "The last thing Abraham needs is to see you driving a motorcycle!"

Selena stopped the bike and climbed off in a hurry. I guess the thought of Abraham was stronger than any other argument I could have given her.

Still, Selena was stubborn enough to think that she knew all about motorcycles after that one little lesson. One night, I came home and saw that my bike was parked crooked in the garage.

I stomped into the house. "Selena? What the hell did you do with my bike?"

"I just took it for a ride through the neighborhood," she said breezily. "It was cool."

I really got into it with her that time. "It was *not* cool! You don't know what could have happened."

I started telling her about my father's accident, then, and about all of my other friends and relatives who'd been left dead or crippled because of some stupid mistake they'd made on their motorcycles. I had to scare her into being sensible.

"Anytime you're tempted to do that again, remember that my dad got dragged for three miles with his motorcycle under a truck," I said.

Selena just stared at me, openmouthed. "That happened to your dad? Shoot," she said. "Okay, I won't take your motorcycle out by myself again."

I almost believed her. Still, I checked on the bike every time I came home after that. I knew how Selena rolled, taking every risk that came her way with courage and joy—in music, in love, and in life.

Around the same time that I got my motorcycle, Selena and I owned two cars. When Selena's charcoal gray BMW M3 was stolen, she took the insurance money and replaced it with a black Porsche 968. I had already given my own car to relatives who needed it and had been sharing the BMW. Since we were on the road so much, it wasn't too much of a hassle to share one vehicle. One day, however, a friend of ours who owned the same dealership where Selena bought her black Porsche convinced us to come and see what he had in his car lot.

"I want to buy something used, not new," I told Selena on the way over to the car dealership. "I don't see the point of buying a new car that will lose its value the minute I drive it off the lot. Let's get something at least a couple of years old."

Selena agreed. No matter how much money she earned in her life, she always remembered her humble start. She still surprised me with stories about how she and her brother and sister had grown up; for instance, she told me that the family never had much money to spend on toys, so the children played mostly with household objects.

"I especially loved playing with clean sheets," Selena told me once. "I liked to make hammocks out of the sheets when they were hanging on the clothesline and lie in them like cocoons."

The minute we pulled into the parking lot of our friend's dealership, I spotted a red Porsche. It was a Targa 911 with a whale tail, the same car that's housed in the Selena museum today. I didn't say anything to Selena, though, because I was wondering if a car that red and conspicuous was really my style. I was pretty sure it wasn't.

We looked at a few BMWs and Porsches. Finally, our friend walked us over to the red car. Right away, Selena said, "Babe, you have to get this one."

I pretended to be busy reading the dealer's information sheet on the car window, despite knowing that, once again, my wife had made up her mind and it would be tough to change it. The car was a 1987 semi-convertible. That removable Targa top was the main reason I bought it—that, and the fact that I could tell right away how much Selena loved the car.

"You know what?" I said. "Let's go do the paperwork."

We bought the car on the spot and drove our two Porsches home on the highway, with her in the black one and me in the red.

Selena frequently told me how much she loved my new car after that. "Your car looks really great," she'd say, sounding a little wistful. "Maybe I should trade my Porsche in for a new one," she'd add once in a while.

"No, no, just keep that car," I'd tell her. "It doesn't make any sense to trade it in now. You just got it."

I loved the red Porsche, but of course Selena drove it now and then. I could see how well it fit her. She'd come in from driving the car around town, her hair blown every which way, and say, 'Man, I love your car.'"

Finally I said, "What do you love about it so much?"

"Everything!" Selena said. "I love the way it handles, and I really like the way people look at me when I'm out there driving in that red car."

I laughed. The truth was, I had been thinking for a while by then about how much we needed another kind of vehicle, maybe a truck. As much as I loved Porsches, they were impractical. There was no way to fit our family of dogs in there, much less any of my guitars and speakers. It would be great to have a truck big enough that we could just toss everything into the back of it. Although we talked about it several times, we were both too busy to actually do anything about it.

A few months went by. As always, we visited my family several times during that period. Selena used to love coming to San Antonio to visit my mom. We often took both cars for the two-hour drive, since once we got there she often went out to do errands to gather materials for her fashion projects. Once we bought the red Porsche, Selena often dared me to race her on the highway between Corpus and San Antonio, even though I always won.

"It's the driver, not the car," I teased her one day as we were setting out to San Antonio. "I'm just a better race car driver than you
are. Admit it."

"Shut up," she said furiously. "I'm a superb driver. The reason
you win is because you're in a better car."

I knew that she was right—the red car was faster, and Selena
was a great driver—but I knew it would make her happy if she got
to prove me wrong.

"Okay," I said one day when I was in an especially generous
mood. "Let's switch cars this time. You take the red one and I'll
drive the black one. We'll see who's faster for real."

Sure enough, the red car left the black one in the dust. "See?"
Selena told me, strutting up the sidewalk.

Finally, on another visit to San Antonio, Selena and I stopped at
a little mom-and-pop grocery store and gas station on the highway.
We were going into the store to buy coffee when an older gentleman
stopped us and pointed at the red 911.

"That's a great car," he said. "What year is it?"

I told him, and we started talking about the Porsche. I glanced
over at Selena, who made a big show of rolling her eyes at me.

Inside the store, Selena came up and slipped her arm through
mine and started giving me a hard time. "You're such a dog," she
said. "That man didn't say anything about *my* car. And you know
what? I don't like my car anymore. It never gets any compliments."

I smiled down at her and paid for the coffee. "I've been thinking.
I don't think that red car is really my style, and I've been considering
this whole truck idea. Wouldn't it be great for us to be able to take
the dogs with us sometimes? We really need a truck for that."

Selena bit her lip, probably to keep from seeming too eager.

"Well, what about the red car?" she asked. "Are you going to trade it in for a truck?"

"Of course not," I said. "I'm going to give it to you."

Selena started jumping up and down. "Are you serious, Chris?"

"Yeah. Let's go looking at trucks when we get back from San Antonio. I'll give you the red car."

She was so excited that she nearly spilled her coffee. Once we were outside the store, she turned me toward her and grabbed my arm. "You know I love you, right?"

"Yeah, I know."

"So can I start driving my car right now?"

Selena made the sad puppy dog face, the same one she always made when she wanted something from me, because she knew that I could never say no to it. So I gave her the keys and that was it. She took off in the red car, and I drove the black one back to San Antonio.

Except that wasn't it, exactly.

Selena headed off in the red Porsche, and I climbed into the black car. We were going to meet up at my mom's for dinner, but Selena planned to run some errands first and I was going to stop at one of my favorite music stores. I had driven maybe a mile when I felt the black Porsche sputtering.

I looked at the gauge, but it said FULL, so I pressed harder on the accelerator, thinking the gauge must be stuck. On the other hand, Selena had a bad habit of running her cars on empty; in fact, I often went out and started her car for her if she had to go somewhere, and I'd check the gas and turn on the heat or air-conditioning so she'd be comfortable in the car right away. I just hadn't thought to do that this time.

Sure enough, I was out of gas. The engine died just as I eased over to the side of the road. I got out and pushed the car into a nearby parking lot, then fished out my cell phone.

When Selena answered, I said, "Hey, I'm over here on the highway and your car just stalled. I could swear it's out of gas. By any chance, do you remember the last time you put gas in your car?"

"Uh, no," she said.

I sighed. "Well, never mind. Come pick me up in your new red car."

Selena and I did go to look at trucks when we returned to San Antonio. There was one that I especially liked, a brand-new 1993 blue Chevy Silverado. Selena loved that truck, too.

"That's a cool-looking truck," she said. "That's you all day."

"I don't know if I want to buy anything new," I said. "Let's think about it."

The car salesman on that lot was an older Mexican-American who recognized Selena right away. He saw us looking over the blue truck and came over to talk about its various features. "You want to take it for a test drive, right?" he said.

When I hesitated, Selena gave me a nudge. "Yeah, okay," I said, and got in.

Selena climbed into the passenger seat. She loved the middle console with the wood trim. Then the salesman leaned over me and lifted up the console, turning the front into a bench seat. Selena took off her seat belt and scooted over next to me.

"Oh, I like this," she said, and started pushing all of the buttons on the dash.

"Me too," I said, laughing. "We'll be gone about ten minutes," I told the salesman.

"Take your time," he said.

Out on the highway, Selena continued to enthusiastically explore the truck's various features. "You've got to get this truck, Chris," she said.

I shook my head. "I want to think about it, Selena. This is a big decision. I'm not like you, always knowing what I want right away."

We drove around Corpus for about half an hour, getting into one of our regular conversations about the future and what we might do if we still had this truck when our kids started arriving.

"Remember that I want five kids," Selena said.

This always made me nervous. "Girl, you have one kid and then we'll talk about it," I joked as I always did. "Plus, if I'm driving this truck, we'll need a minivan, too. No more Porsche for you."

When we returned to the dealer's lot, the salesman came out to greet us. "How did you like it?"

Selena said, "We loved it!"

"It's a cool truck," I agreed, then gave Selena a warning look. "But I want to think about it."

A few days later, I still hadn't made up my mind. We had been busy, and now it was our first wedding anniversary. Abraham and Marcella were holding a big party for us in their backyard; they had set up a tent and everything because we were expecting so many people.

Selena was running late, as usual. She was taking forever to get dressed and do her hair and makeup. I did what I usually did while I waited for her: played my guitar in the living room, trying to work out a new song.

There was a knock on the door, and when I went to answer it, I was surprised to see A.B. Unlike Abraham, who stopped by the house whenever the mood struck, A.B. hardly ever came over without calling. Besides, we were going to see him in just a few minutes at the party.

"Hey, what's up?" I said.

"You getting ready for the party?" A.B. asked.

"Yeah, I'm waiting for your sister as usual," I said.

"Well, I've got to run to the store. Why don't you come with me?"

This was weird, I thought, since A.B. had never in his life stopped by to invite me to go buy something at any store. "What do you need to get?" I asked suspiciously.

"I need to get some gum," he said.

"Okay," I said with a shrug. This still seemed strange to me. On the other hand, I was getting restless waiting for Selena.

"Selena?" I called. "I'm going with A.B. to the store. I'll get more beer for the party while I'm at it."

As we took off for the store, a blue truck came around the corner. It was almost dark; I watched the truck pass us, but didn't really get a good look at it in the dusky light.

"I think that was like the truck I told you about, the one Selena and I were thinking about buying," I said.

"Yeah? I didn't see it. Sorry," A.B. said.

At the store, A.B. bought his gum and I got some beer. Then we drove back to my house to pick up Selena for the party.

The blue Silverado truck was parked in our driveway. "Happy anniversary, baby!" Selena cried.

I was shocked almost speechless. I couldn't believe that she had gone back to the dealer, put a down payment on the truck and done all of the paperwork herself.

I laughed and hugged her. "Let's go for a ride."

No matter how well I thought I knew her, Selena always managed to surprise me. One day, I came home to a garage that reeked suspiciously of gasoline and some kind of small engine stink, like a lawn mower. It took me a minute to pinpoint the source: there was a go-kart in our garage.

I went into the house and called for Selena. When she didn't answer, I tried her cell phone. "Hey, Selena, what's this go-kart doing in our garage?"

"Oh, yeah," she said. "I bought a go-kart today."

"You bought a go-kart? Just like that?" I wasn't angry or anything. Just surprised, I told her.

"Yeah," she said again. "I always wanted a go-kart when I was a kid. Didn't you?"

That was one thing Selena and I definitely shared: a love of vehicles, especially the kind that could give you a thrill when you were driving them. I laughed and said, "Big toys for big people, right?"

"Right," she said. "I'm on my way home. I'll tell you the rest of the story when I get there."

What had happened was this: Selena had been driving around Corpus in her car with our friend Nicolette, a singer who had been with Los Dinos for a little while. The two of them had driven past a dealer that sold ATVs, and there was a whole line of go-karts parked in the lot next to the road. Selena had pulled over and bought one of them then and there. The dealer had delivered the go-kart to the house on the very same day.

Selena started laughing then, telling me in the kitchen how the neighborhood kids had seen her and Nicolette driving the go-kart over to the school in our neighborhood. Selena let the kids all have a turn driving it. "Nicolette, though, she was hogging that go-kart and trying to show off her driving," Selena said. "She was driving really fast and doing doughnuts in the school yard and everything."

She really started to crack up then, laughing so hard that tears started streaming down her face. For a minute she couldn't even speak because she was gasping for breath.

"What?" I asked. "What happened?"

"Nicolette comes tearing right by me, takes a turn on the grass, and falls off!" she said. "She wasn't buckled in, so her butt slid right off the seat and she went rolling over and over!"

"Is she okay?" I said, but I was laughing by now, too, picturing this.

"Sure, she's fine, but that dummy was trying to be slick with the thing and look what happened," Selena said, wiping her eyes.

"What about you? Did you fall off?" I asked. "Are you okay?"

Selena gave me one of those looks. "Of course I'm fine. You know me. I can drive whatever."

It was true, too. I'd seen her do it. From motorcycles to fast cars, from go-karts to trucks, Selena loved a fast ride, the wilder the better.

On February 3, 1993, Selena y Los Dinos performed at the Memorial Coliseum in Corpus Christi. Located on the bay, the Coliseum was built in honor of World War II veterans from Corpus. This building, which was unfortunately demolished in 2010, was an incredible place to perform mainly because of the enormous curved steel roof with its thin concrete cover—the world's largest unsupported span when it was built.

We loved performing anywhere in Corpus, really, because we could get ready at home and didn't have to rush, other than me trying to work around Selena in the bathroom. Tonight she was throwing a party at the house—just close friends and family—but the problem was that by now so many fans knew where we lived. They sometimes knew more about our schedule than we did.

We never had anyone act rude or offensive; at the most, fans might drive by our house with horns blaring, with one of Selena's songs blasting from their speakers, or yelling out the window. This happened constantly after our shows in Corpus, so we kept the party a secret until after we were through playing that night.

Another secret—to me, that is—was the fact that we were planning to record the concert for the next album—the album that would eventually be titled *Selena Live!* It was probably best that I didn't realize, since I was already feeling nervous about what kind of turnout we'd have, given that the Coliseum was the biggest performance venue in Corpus. I was also concerned about getting the sound check done and whether my gear would work. Selena y Los Dinos wasn't a small family any longer; our productions now required a caravan of three eighteen-wheeler semitrucks carrying the band, the road crew, and our equipment. Nothing was as simple as it used to be.

When we arrived at the Coliseum, Selena and I were amazed by the number of cars in the parking lot. Over three thousand local fans had turned up for the show, but somehow the Coliseum officials had still managed to set things up to accommodate dancing, in true Tejano fashion.

I went onstage to check things out. Selena, meanwhile, went straight to the dressing room backstage, where she sorted through her clothing and made some last-minute costume decisions.

Suddenly I heard an announcement that we should all dress in our stage gear and assemble for a photograph that would appear on the album cover—and that's when it dawned on me that this show would be our next album. Apparently, the decision to record the show had been made a long time ago, but I had never heard.

I didn't bother asking questions. I just made sure that Selena and I were dressed and in the right place at the right time. This was one of those situations where Abraham would pull me aside to say, "Listen, don't let Selena be late."

"I'll do my best," I told him, which was pretty much my standard response. I knew that I didn't have any more control over Selena than he did; the difference was that this didn't bother me.

The show went well, but afterward I started to worry because I thought I had messed up quite a few times. In my mind, I went over and over the mistakes, and decided I'd have to fix them when we went into the studio to finish mixing the album. As it turned out, there were just two chords that needed to be fixed.

Selena, though, had a great time from start to finish. The weird thing about playing in your hometown is that you always worry nobody will show up, because everyone already knows you and has heard your music over and over again. Selena was ecstatic that night about having drawn so many fans and to have had such a fantastic audience for the show. She also knew that the crowd's energy would transform the new album.

As planned, the band came over to our house after the show. It was a terrific party. What I remember most about that evening, though, is going into the bedroom after everyone else had left. Selena had gone to bed before me; I still had to let the dogs out and lock up the house.

"Hey," I said, surprised to see the light still on in the bedroom. "What are you doing still up?"

She smiled at me. "Just relaxing," she said. "Reading." She picked up the fashion magazine off her knees and showed it to me. "Great show, huh?"

"Yeah," I said, but I wasn't thinking about the show or the party. I was marveling at my wife.

We had played well and entertained thousands of people. Now here was Selena, sharing my bed and looking as beautiful as she always did, just relaxing and reading like any other woman. She looked so down to earth and calm. How was that possible, after the energy she had expended to perform onstage? And how had I gotten so lucky, to be able to share these miraculous moments with her?

I got into bed with Selena and we talked a little more about the show. "I didn't even know we were going to record it," I admitted finally.

She laughed. "I told you, dummy. So did A.B."

"I must not have been paying attention," I said, and it was true: most of the time, I was paying attention to Selena. She already held a place deep in my heart, and I was falling more in love with her with each day that passed.

Selena's gradual rise to popularity became a meteor ride in 1993 after the release of *Selena Live!*, which was our fourth album for EMI Latin and featured the live recording of Selena's concert hits as well as three new tracks: "No Debes Jugar," "La Llamada," and "Tú Robaste Mi Corazón." Those three singles rapidly rose to be named among the top five hits on the U.S. Hot Latin Tracks chart, and the album itself was certified Gold on the charts.

Shortly after the Corpus concert, the fact that Selena had become a major Latin attraction was confirmed when we played at the Houston Livestock Show and Rodeo in the Astrodome with David Lee Garza. Together, we drew nearly sixty thousand people, an audience that no Tejano act had ever managed to attract to that event before. Selena also won Female Vocalist of the Year and Female Entertainer of the Year at the Tejano Music Awards that year, as well as Album of the Year for *Entre a Mi Mundo*.

This success definitely didn't go unnoticed by the record labels—in November, Selena y Los Dinos agreed to make an English-language record with SBK Records. One of our biggest supporters, Daniel Glass, the CEO of the EMI Records Group, compared Selena to Madonna in his interview with *Billboard* magazine, saying, "She has that same control, and I love artists that know where they want to go and how to get there. She's definitely a pop star."

Behind the scenes, Selena was excited about her success, but uncertain at times as well. She was loyal to her fan base and didn't want to disappoint people by singing only in English. She intended to keep making Tejano music.

More worrisome to her was what might happen to her family and the band if she continued on this path to international stardom. One day, I boarded the bus to find Selena lying in her bunk and looking really depressed. Nothing bad had happened, but I could tell that she was out of it, almost in a daze.

"You okay?" I rested my hand on her forehead to see if she had a fever because her usual bright gaze was dull, but her face was cool. "You don't look right."

"Yeah, I'm okay," she said.

"Sure?"

"Yeah, I'm sure."

I gave her a kiss and walked on by, continuing to move my guitars onto the bus and into a closet. When I'd finished, I went back to the bunks to check on her. She was still lying there in the same position.

I sat down on the floor next to her. "Selena, what's going on? What are you thinking about?"

She sighed. "I'm thinking about the mainstream English album."

"Are you nervous?"

"No, I'm not nervous," she said. "That's not it."

I tried to reassure her anyway. "It'll be fine, you know. Look at the hard work we did for the Latin side. It won't be as hard as it was when we played in Mexico the first time, and you succeeded there. You're doing great. You won't have to worry about anything. You'll be an American artist, same as you are now, only you'll be singing in English over and over again just like you're singing in Spanish over and over again now."

This made Selena laugh. "I know," she said. "I know it'll be a lot of work, but I can do it."

"Right," I said. "You've never been afraid of working hard, and you're going to be great." I watched her for a minute, alarmed because I saw that Selena was on the verge of tears.

"Tell me," I said. "Please talk to me. Why are you so sad?"

She shuddered a little and turned on her side to face me. A tear slid down one cheek and her voice was hardly over a whisper. I needed to lean closer to her to hear the words.

"It's just that I was thinking about what it'll be like when I have to go and do those concerts in English," she said. "The music is so different from Tejano. You're probably the only musician in the band who can play pop songs. A.B. is already saying that he can't go because he's not that kind of bass player. Suzette can't play drums like that, because she doesn't know how to play drums for pop music. Los Dinos won't cut it in the mainstream."

I took Selena's hand but couldn't say anything. I knew that she was right. I just hadn't thought about this before. I had grown up playing rock music and pop music, and I was a good enough guitar player to learn anything off a record.

I knew that I could play the music the label wanted us to do for a mainstream English-language album. The other guys couldn't, other than Ricky, probably, but that wasn't where his heart was. If Selena was going to stay at the top of her game and make it in the mainstream commercial music world, she needed to be backed by a band as tight and sophisticated as Mariah Carey's or Whitney Houston's. She didn't have that in Los Dinos.

"So what do you want to do?" I asked. "Do you want to not make the album?"

Selena cried harder, hearing this. "I already signed the contract. Besides, you know I want to make it. But I just don't know if I can be singing onstage, turn around, and not have A.B. and Suzette up there with me. It's not going to be the same."

"No," I agreed. "It won't be the same." I took a deep breath, then asked, "Are you telling me that, if you'd thought of this before, you would have told them you wouldn't make the English album?"

Selena looked me in the eyes and nodded. "Yes. That's what I would have said."

I was conflicted. I knew that Selena wanted to succeed on an international level—that's what she had worked so hard for all her life—but I also understood her enduring loyalty and love for her family.

"Everything is going to be fine," I said at last, even though I only partly believed this. "Suzette can take drum lessons and A.B. can start stretching himself on the bass. They can learn. And we'll still play some Spanish songs with the other guys for more Tejano albums, too."

"You really think we can make it work?" Selena asked.

"We can try," I said. "That's all anybody can do, right?"

Selena Live! came out on May 4, 1993, shortly after Selena gave me the truck for our first wedding anniversary. When it was nominated for a Grammy, none of us could believe it, despite all of our recent successes. Selena and I flew to New York with Suzette, A.B. and his wife for the awards ceremony in Radio City Music Hall. Of course we were all excited to be nominated, but I don't think any of us ever imagined that we might actually win.

Selena and I were mainly thrilled to have a chance to meet some of the performers we admired, or at least see them perform in person. I was particularly looking forward to seeing Sting, but the one Selena couldn't wait to see was Whitney Houston, who was one of her favorite singers.

As our plane began its descent over the Manhattan skyline, I looked past Selena and out the window. The Twin Towers loomed in the distance, and I couldn't believe how tall they were. I thought those must be the buildings that King Kong had climbed on in the movies I'd watched as a kid. We could see the Statue of Liberty, too, small but gleaming in the distance, and a tingle of excitement ran up my spine. I couldn't believe that I was finally going to see New York City.

We took a limo from the airport to a hotel around the corner from Radio City Music Hall. As Selena and I stepped out onto the sidewalk in front of the hotel, we were immediately assaulted by the smells, the blaring car horns, and the crowds of people. New York was nothing like Corpus, or even San Antonio.

Selena entered the hotel ahead of me. As I moved to follow her into the lobby, an angry altercation broke out on the street as a taxi driver got out of his car and started yelling and swearing at another driver, who came over and banged on the taxi's hood with his fist.

I must have come inside in a hurry and with some weird expression on my face, because Selena said, "Everything okay, Chris?"

"I don't know," I said. "These two guys were fighting outside. A taxicab driver and some other guy."

"Don't go back out there alone," she advised.

I immediately agreed. We had seen New York City in the movies, but it seemed like the people here were even crazier than they seemed on film.

The awards show wasn't until that night. Abraham had arranged for Selena to have meetings with record label executives that day, so she went to those with A.B. and then went shopping with Suzette.

I did end up braving the New York City streets alone, meanwhile, and bought some gear I couldn't find in Texas.

For the show, Selena wore a floor-length beaded white dress with a fishtail hem in the back. She was really nervous by then, and kept losing her temper with me because the back of the dress dragged on the floor and I kept walking too close to her and stepping on it by mistake.

"Back up a little bit, Chris," she whispered at one point. "It's hard enough to walk in this thing. If you step on the hem, I'm going to fall down, and I sure don't want to do that right here in front of everybody."

We all sat together in the Radio City Music Hall theater. When Selena's name was called as the Grammy winner in the Best Mexican-American album category, we all jumped up out of our seats and cheered.

"Oh, Chris!" Selena whispered to me. "I can't believe I won!"

I gave her a hug and then nudged her. "Come on, come on. You've got to go down there and make your speech!"

"What if I fall on this dress? Oh, please don't let me trip and fall on the way down there," I heard her murmur as she made her way out to the aisle and started toward the stage.

Selena didn't trip, and she had never looked more beautiful than that night in her beaded white dress, with her hair tamed into an elegant updo, as she gave her brief speech thanking Jose Behar, the band, and all of her family members.

After the speech, Selena was whisked away backstage while the rest of us enjoyed watching the remainder of the show. Selena had been so starstruck by the idea of meeting other artists at the Grammys that she had brought a camera to take pictures of herself with them; unfortunately, they hadn't allowed us to bring the cameras into the theater, so I knew that she must be feeling frustrated backstage. Besides, I thought with a grin, Selena would be the one that everyone would want pictures of now, since she was one of the winners.

As we left Radio City Music Hall that night, we heard people screaming Selena's name outside. She couldn't believe they knew her name. But she was still cool, waving at all of them like she was the First Lady or something, even though that whole time she was worrying about falling on that dress.

Then it was over, and Selena could say that she had won a Grammy. It's funny how winning a Grammy doesn't seem like such a big deal until you win it—and then it's a very big deal indeed, mainly because you've been recognized by the music industry and other doors begin opening up to new opportunities all around you, simply because you've earned the industry's nod of approval.

For A.B., too, this was a big day. He had been trying to get people to pay attention to his production quality, and at the end of the day, he was recognized as a great producer. We were all parts of his puzzle, but he was the one who had put the pieces together.

Many thought of Selena as a solo artist—the name "Los Dinos" had even been dropped from the front of her albums by the time she won the Grammy, and we were credited only on the back—yet I knew that every time we put out a new record, other groups were now trying to imitate our sounds, and would be for a long time to come. Selena was right: all of us had come to rely upon one another as family, and it was important for us to stick together.

ELEVEN

DREAMS COME TRUE

$\mathcal{A}$braham had once called me "a cancer" in the Quintanilla family. I turned out to be benign. Nobody detected the real cancer, which appeared in the form of a short, homely woman named Yolanda Saldivar.

I first met Yolanda shortly before Selena and I were married, when we were still seeing each other on the down low. My first memories of Yolanda are vague. I used to see her at some of our shows, usually in San Antonio. Occasionally she would be on the bus, too, visiting with Selena and Suzette. Once I became acquainted with her, I might say, "Hey, what's up?" if I walked by Yolanda at a show or on the bus, but that was it.

Beyond that, everything I knew about Yolanda at first was hearsay. To me, she was just another friend of the Quintanilla family—a friend whom everyone seemed to like and trust. I was polite to her but that was as far as our relationship went in those early years.

I had heard somewhere that Yolanda, a registered nurse, attended one of Selena's concerts in 1991, and was apparently so entranced by Selena's music that she had approached Suzette, who was in charge of Selena's merchandising. Yolanda had proposed starting a fan club in San Antonio.

I hadn't paid much attention to this story at the time. Selena had so many fans, and by the time Selena and I were a couple, Yolanda seemed to do a great job as her fan club president, rapidly adding members in the San Antonio area. Members could pay to belong to the fan club and receive T-shirts, posters, and other souvenirs in exchange for their membership fee. Or, they could belong for free, and receive a monthly newsletter with a schedule of where we were playing.

Yolanda seemed to live for her job as Selena's fan club president. She was older than we were, and acted very sincere and professional. She seemed to want nothing more than to help Selena in any way she could, acting maternal toward her at first, very sweet and caring.

What none of us knew at the time is that Yolanda had first approached Shelly Lares, whom I had played with before joining Los Dinos, with the same kind of proposition. Shelly's father, Fred, had turned Yolanda down. Shelly was the one who initially introduced Yolanda to Suzette.

We also had no idea that Yolanda had a history of legal troubles. She had defaulted on her student loan and one of her employers, a dermatologist, had sued Yolanda in 1983, claiming that she had stolen money from his business.

Why did Abraham, usually so cautious, trust Yolanda? Probably because Yolanda seemed so harmless and played her cards just right. She was sweet, very soft-spoken, and extremely respectful toward Abraham. Suzette had introduced Yolanda to him, and he liked the idea of having someone outside the family manage the fan club, since the rest of them were so overwhelmed. Yolanda proved to be especially useful in San Antonio, where we often stayed to work in the studio or play in shows. The Quintanillas and the band all came by bus, so Suzette and Selena were stranded unless Yolanda took them to run errands in her car.

For whatever reasons, Abraham, usually so mistrustful of outsiders, welcomed Yolanda into the inner circle of people who were known and trusted by the Quintanillas.

"Fan clubs can ruin you if things aren't run the right way and people don't get the items or the newsletter they were promised," Selena explained to me. "I'm so glad that Yolanda is running things the way she is. The fan club keeps growing and everybody's really happy."

To show how grateful she was to Yolanda, Selena often gave her gifts. Yolanda seemed to have a thing for spotted cows, for instance, so Selena bought her an expensive rug with a cow on it. She also bought her a cow phone on a trip to Los Angeles. Slowly, Yolanda was becoming closer to Suzette and Selena, who both treated her like another sister. When it was time to make Selena's big dream come true, then, it seemed natural for Selena to call upon her good friend for help.

Whether she was at home with me or on the road, Selena was always sketching fashion designs and making clothing and accessories with her own hands. She had loved fashion since childhood, and took delight in her bag of metal, glue, pliers, and costume jewelry; she was always working on a new belt or jazzing up her stage outfits at the last minute.

Things had already been going well for the band. Now, after winning the Grammy, it was like one of those lawn mowers that you pull to start, and it doesn't want to start. You keep at it, though, and the lawn mower sputters and stops, sputters and stops, until all of a sudden you get it and the lawn mower zooms off. That's how it felt for us. There was always something that needed to be done, and that thing would be linked to something else, which was linked again to another thing we were asked to do.

It was incredible how much we were traveling and playing, how many albums and singles we were selling, and how much everyone loved Selena. Her appeal went far beyond what she did musically. For instance, Selena recorded a Public Service Announcement for a battered women's shelter. Every time a radio station aired this tape, "Put an End to the Pain," the phones lit up with Spanish callers who had heard Selena's voice and decided to improve their own lives by seeking help for themselves.

Selena never took any of this adoration for granted. She was always humble, and worried constantly that she might not be working hard enough. She was Abraham's daughter, no question about that—she had his drive and work ethic, coupled with a creative spark all her own.

In late 1993, the Quintanilla family decided to use their new credibility and improved financial position to start Q Productions, a production company and recording studio of their own in a former body shop near the airport in Corpus Christi. Abraham had always wanted to have a world-class studio close to home, and he envisioned eventually heading up his own label. He managed that company while A.B. formed the Phat Kat Groove production company.

Both Abraham and A.B. were interested in producing the work of new artists, mainstream commercial groups as well as Tejano, and expanding the Quintanilla music dynasty. Selena soon followed with a business of her own in January 1994, when she finally opened the boutiques she had talked about for so long.

Abraham was fit to be tied when he heard about Selena's decision. "What is wrong with you?" he asked, shaking his head. "How could you even think about opening another business? Do you know how much time that will take and how much harder you're making your life? Why don't you just enjoy the money you're making?"

Selena held firm. "It's what I want to do, Dad," she said. "And it's my life."

Still not willing to give up on dissuading his daughter, Abraham pulled me aside next. "You can't let her do this," he said desperately. "She'll burn herself out."

"I get why you're worried about her biting off more than she can chew," I said gently. "But this is something she really wants to do, and I'm not going to tell Selena no. If anything, I'll do whatever I have to do to help her."

Despite his own ambitious nature, Abraham thought that Selena was making a huge mistake. He couldn't really stop her, though. Selena and I were financially independent and, as I had already realized, Abraham never really did control Selena as much as other people thought he did, especially after she married me.

I think some people may have had the mistaken impression that Abraham dictated every aspect of Selena's life because she often relied on him to run interference for her. If someone came to her with an idea that didn't thrill her, she would say, "That sounds interesting, but you need to talk to my dad."

TO *Selena*, WITH LOVE

This happened many times as Selena got more popular and more people tried to convince her to invest in one thing or another that they were working on. "I'll have to run it by my dad," she would say, but that was simply her way of ending the conversation.

So, when Selena came to me one night and said, "Okay, Chris. I'm ready to open my boutique. I don't want to wait anymore. Let's go shopping for a building," I knew there was nothing that Abraham could do to dissuade her. As I had told Abraham, I would help her any way I could—but first I had to be sure that Selena knew what kind of work was involved.

"You're going to be busier than you already are," I reminded her. "And you already don't have enough hours in the day."

"We can do it," she promised. "I'm not going to do all of the work. I'll get people to help me."

"You really want this, huh?" I asked.

"What do you think?" She made a face at me. "You've only been listening to me talk about this for two years, but I've wanted a boutique of my own since I was a little kid."

"Okay, then," I said. "Let's get it going."

Truthfully, I would have been cool just being a musician. I didn't need or want to open another business. What I knew about the fashion business you could write on the head of a pin. But there was nothing in the world that Selena wanted more than this. I also figured that, even if Selena wound up discovering that owning a fashion boutique didn't live up to her fantasy or suit her lifestyle, at the very least she would have had a chance to get the idea out of her system.

Selena and I started scoping out commercial buildings for lease or for sale all over Corpus. At last we found the right place: a 1950s frame house at 4926 Everhart. We loved the building because of its classic style. The location was perfect, too, close to Corpus Christi's biggest shopping centers, which had been built in the past decade. The building was for sale at a good price, and there were new businesses springing up all around it.

"This area has great potential," Selena said, and I agreed.

We went down to the bank and did the paperwork to finance the sale, then started looking around for a contractor. Once we'd settled on a contractor recommended by one of our friends, Selena began drawing pictures of what she wanted the boutique to look like.

This was one of those times when Selena most appreciated my help, I think. I had grown up around a stepfather who was very handy around the house; I'd helped him renovate rooms and do an addition on the house I grew up in, so I knew some handyman basics. Selena would describe her ideas to me as she sketched them out, and I'd help her get these ideas across to the contractor.

I had never seen Selena more excited than when she started playing around with her building plans and talking about the interior details for her boutique. She envisioned selling her own fashion designs here, and having an in-house salon where clients could get their hair and nails done.

After the contractor had finished the major part of the renovations, Selena and I went in and did some of the finish work. "I really want there to be a lot of light in here," Selena explained, pointing out the way she wanted to place windows between the manicure stations.

To satisfy her request, I ended up installing glass block walls between the manicure stations, which were arranged in a zigzag fashion along a big table. I had to go out and buy a kit to figure out how to make the glass walls, but in the end I managed.

Her mom was the only member of the family who supported Selena's dream as immediately and completely as I did. "Selena has wanted to do this ever since she was a little girl," she told me. "I'm so glad she's got you to help her."

Marcella made these crazy-looking vines that I put up around the top of the salon. I also bought a high-end sound system so that Selena could have high-quality sound in her boutique, and ran the wires so that nothing would show.

It took several months for us to secure the building permits and complete the remodeling. Selena then did the hiring process herself because she wanted to handpick the women who would staff her boutique. She had also met a young Texan fashion designer, Martin Gomez, who agreed to help her transform the designs she visualized in her mind, and in two dimensions as sketches on paper, into exciting, three-dimensional clothes and accessories. Selena's overall goal was to make the kinds of dramatic outfits and accessories that she liked to wear onstage or for a night out—and sell these to the public at affordable prices.

Selena even designed the tags that would be sewn into the clothing—just a small thing, a label on a piece of clothing, but again, it was her very own and it looked professional. To think of something and dream about it for so long, and then to realize that dream, is an incredible accomplishment for anyone. To Selena it was the definition of happiness.

I was constantly amazed by her energy and attention to detail as Selena got her new venture off the ground, especially because she was still performing nonstop and keeping up her contractual agreements with sponsors like Coca-Cola and Agree shampoo. At the same time, Selena never forgot where her heart was—she was still making time to do charity work, like speaking to children in schools about the importance of education in various "Stay in School" jamborees.

During one visit to a local middle school, for instance, I sat in the audience while Selena went up to the podium. Microphone in hand, she looked earnestly at her young audience—kids who were the same age she was when she started in the music business as a singer—and told them straight up not to follow her path, but to stay in school.

"Music isn't a very stable business," she said. "It comes and goes, and so does money. But your education stays with you." "If you have a dream," Selena added, "don't ever let anybody take that away from you. The impossible is always possible."

The kids went wild, especially when Selena sang for them. Then she went down off the stage and stood among the middle school students. She autographed anything and everything they handed her, with a kind personal word for each child.

It was an exhausting time, a truly wild ride. Yet, being beside Selena every step of the way, and watching the look of pleasure on her face as we successfully hurdled every obstacle, from gutting the place to painting the walls and hanging the neon sign with her name on it, made our efforts worthwhile to me. Together, with hard work and determination, we brought her dream to life.

"It looks awesome," I said, putting my arm around Selena's waist as we gazed up at that newly hung neon sign with her SELENA, ETC. logo. "Man, you're really doing this! It's really happening."

"Thank you, Chris," she said, putting her head on my shoulder and gazing happily up at her name in lights.

After Selena had opened the boutique in Corpus Christi, she decided that it would make sense to have a second salon and shop in San Antonio, the other city where we spent most of our time, and where she had another great fan base. In addition, my sister and other friends of ours would be able to staff the San Antonio boutique.

About eight months after we opened the Corpus boutique, Selena opened the second one on Broadway in San Antonio—coincidentally, about a block and a half from the apartment where I had lived with my dad while Selena and I were dating. Because we were already so busy, this venture was more businesslike than a labor of love; we hired people to complete the work we needed done inside and out, rather than trying to take that on ourselves.

At the same time that Selena's boutiques began gaining traction, her career as an entertainer was moving at an even faster clip. She was busier than ever in 1994. Now her obligations included making music videos—the new industry standard—as well as recording vocals.

For instance, the music video for "La Llamada," one of Selena's biggest hits from the *Selena Live!* album, was shot on the rooftop of a beach house in Malibu, California, which meant that we all had to fly out there for two days.

Many of the scenes in that video are of Selena singing with a crowd of people dancing around her, as if she's at a big party; shooting them was fairly uneventful. We just had to spend a day playing through the songs over and over again, and then Los Dinos got to leave. Selena, however, had to stay for several more hours, because they were also shooting her singing the song against a blue curtain.

At one point, I went back up to the roof to see how she was doing. I was worried because the sun was going down. The darker it got, the colder and windier it got, and Selena was wearing only a slim-fitting black dress that couldn't be very warm.

I found her with a blanket around her shoulders between shots. Still, Selena's teeth were starting to chatter and she was shivering. I put my arms around her, rubbing her shoulders to try to warm her up a little.

"How are you doing?" I asked.

"I'm freezing," she said.

"Yeah, I can tell. I don't think we have any jackets."

"I know," she said miserably.

"Want me to stay up here with you?"

"No, no, I'm almost done," she said.

"Let me get you some coffee at least," I said, and went off to find one of the assistants.

They started shooting the video again as I made my way down from the roof. When I turned to watch, I saw that the blanket had come off Selena's shoulders and, as she sang her heart out, she looked totally happy and warm. Selena was a natural actress who was professional enough to slip into a new mood as easily as most people put on a new outfit.

Having so many obligations like that pulling at her made Selena start depending even more on Yolanda Saldivar. Yolanda had done nothing to cause us to mistrust her at this point. In fact, in her un-paid position as Selena's San Antonio fan club president, Yolanda had worked hard to impress everyone in the family with her work ethic and commitment to Selena and the Quintanilla family.

Yolanda had even moved to Corpus Christi in 1993 and rented an apartment with a roommate in order to live closer to the Quintanillas; little did we know that her roommate had moved out within a few months as Yolanda proceeded to turn the apartment into a shrine to Selena. All I saw was that Yolanda had become a close friend to both Suzette and Selena. She had also become Selena's personal assistant, doing everything from helping her out with costume changes backstage to running interference between Selena and overzealous fans.

The more trustworthy Yolanda seemed, the more trusting we all were with her. It was only natural, then, for Selena to offer Yolanda an official, paid position as a manager who would oversee both the clothing boutique in Corpus and the store in San Antonio. The stores had local managers on-site—in fact, my sister, Tricia, was managing the San Antonio boutique—". . . but, if I can't be there to do something, I'll feel better knowing that Yolanda will take care of it," Selena told me.

I agreed with her decision. Selena was trying to juggle too much in her life and Yolanda had proven her loyalty. Abraham, too, thought the idea made sense; he was relieved to have any amount of stress lifted off his daughter's shoulders. Yolanda was put on salary, and Selena gave her a credit card and a cell phone she could use for business purposes. The more support Selena got for her new venture, the better, I thought. I was already out of my depth with the business and I just wanted my wife to be happy.

Everything went smoothly at first. If something needed to be done at one of the boutiques, Yolanda would either handle it or call us while we were on the road. Or, if Selena was in Corpus, Yolanda would help with her calendar. She seemed to diminish the intense pressure that Selena had been feeling since opening the boutiques, and for that we were all grateful.

As the months went by, Selena increasingly relied on Yolanda for assistance, especially once she started thinking seriously about opening up a third boutique where most of her fan base was, in Monterrey, Mexico. We didn't know anything about managing a business. Yolanda didn't either, but she acted like she knew, and we started leaning on her more and more. We were eager to be independent of Abraham, and besides, Yolanda had personal connections in Monterrey and was always willing to drive down there with Selena to explore business prospects.

I didn't really see Yolanda much. If I happened to drop Selena off at the boutique in Corpus for her to get her hair and nails done, I'd chat with Yolanda for a few minutes. That was pretty much the extent of my interactions with her, other than occasional lunches with Yolanda and Selena, where they would talk about business or people they knew and I'd crack a joke here and there.

I never saw Yolanda as a threat. She was like all of those girls in high school I used to feel sorry for because they seemed to have no lives of their own. There was no reason to ever suspect that she was dangerous. In a weird way, I think that all of us were probably even more accepting of her than we might have been if Yolanda had been another kind of woman—pretty or ambitious or clever—because we were so determined to judge her not by her looks or talents, but by where her heart was.

I will regret every day I live that I was so blind. In my defense, I was young. I was in love. I had friends and a wife I adored. I was making music in a band that was increasingly successful and I was making plenty of money. The way I saw things, Selena and I had a bright future ahead of us. My main concern was that Selena was as happy as I was, and that seemed to be true.

There was just one small thing that, looking back on it, probably should have been a red flag. It happened at one of our annual band parties.

Soon after I became involved with Selena, Yolanda started arranging annual parties for the band members, their families, and close friends every year. Selena and I loved those parties. We thought it was cool to hang out in a restaurant or some other regular place with everybody together; ironically, because our band was always working, it was difficult for us to find much time to socialize together.

Gradually, as the years passed, however, I started to sense a growing distance and even a weird vibe between Yolanda and some of the other people at the parties. I didn't know it at the time, but Yolanda had started taking her role as Selena's personal assistant to the next level; people who wanted to reach Selena would increasingly have to get around Yolanda first. Suzette would stand up for Yolanda if anyone complained about her, though, and Selena herself would say, "Send them to Yolanda," if someone wanted to see her and Selena was too busy, which was often the case.

Anyway, at one of these band parties, the restaurant bathroom was vandalized, and Selena heard from Yolanda that I had been involved in it with some other guys.

Remembering the way I had gotten drunk and trashed that hotel room the year before our marriage no doubt made Selena even more suspicious. "Did you trash that bathroom, Chris?" she asked. "Yolanda says you did."

"No," I said. "You know I couldn't have done that. Selena, you know where I was. We were together the whole time."

"Oh. Okay," Selena said, and we moved on to talk about something else.

The conversation didn't really register with me at the time. Because of the band's success, Selena and I were always swatting away silly rumors. Maybe that's why I didn't see this conversation for what it really was: a warning sign that Yolanda was trying to come between Selena and me, the same way that she was trying to make sure that Selena didn't get too close to anyone else.

Despite Yolanda's attempts to make trouble between us and the increased pressure that came with being more successful, Selena and I were more in love than ever. We worked as a team whether we were taking care of our dogs or our house. In everything we did, I tried to follow the advice a friend gave me before I got married.

"I don't think a relationship can ever work if each person gives just fifty percent," he had said.

"Why not?" I asked, puzzled. "That sounds fair to me."

He shook his head. "No, the real way to think about marriage is that you have to each give one hundred percent."

Selena and I both gave one hundred percent to each other. We never kept score the way some couples we knew did, with a "you did that, so I'm going to do this," kind of tally. We had no pet peeves with each other. We were best friends.

For instance, in the same way that Selena had always dreamed about opening her own fashion boutiques, she knew that my goal since high school had been to become a songwriter who produced music on my own. Even though Selena had been adamant about me staying with Los Dinos so that I could be on the road with her, she did everything she could to support me in reaching this goal.

By the time Selena opened her boutiques, Abraham had started to manage different bands through Q Productions. When he found a rock band in Corpus that he wanted to take on, he asked if I'd like to write some songs for them. The idea didn't sound appealing to me—if I'd wanted to form a rock band or even write music for one, it wouldn't have been with these particular musicians. But I decided to do it because I wanted to help Abraham, and maybe I would learn something in the process.

One day, the singer of this band came over to work on a song I'd written, with lyrics by Ricky. Selena was there, wearing one of the bandannas she always used to tie up her hair when she was dusting and vacuuming at home. She cleaned the house while this singer and I worked for hours on a song in our home studio. I had no idea that Selena was actively listening as I kept trying to teach the guy to do the song a certain way, putting emphasis here or there on the lyrics and hitting certain notes. But he just couldn't get it; he never really understood what I meant. Finally, frustrated, I told him we were through for the day.

"Let's just pick this up tomorrow," I said.

The second I had walked him out the door, Selena was standing right beside me. "Babe, how did you not lose your mind with that guy, going over and over that song?" she asked.

I laughed. "Not every singer is as good as you are," I said. "I wish they were. But your dad really wants me to do this."

"I can sing it," she said. "Let me sing it for you."

I thought she was joking. "Why would you want to do that?"

"I know what you want," she said. "I was listening to you this whole time."

"The whole time?" I asked in disbelief.

216

"Yes, the whole time. And I want to sing that song. I like what you wrote," she said. "Please can I sing it?"

I felt awkward, truthfully. Here was the superstar Selena, who just happened to be my wife, and she wanted to sing my demo! On the other hand, I couldn't resist hearing what she could do with my song.

"You know what?" I said. "Let's go."

We both put on headphones and I turned my back as I started up the machines on the mixing board. As soon as the music started, she said, "Okay, I'm going to sing it," and she did.

Selena nailed that song the first time through from beginning to end, exactly the way I'd been describing it to the other singer. At the end of the song, she added even more to it.

I was in shock. How was it possible that I could be so lucky? Selena had been supportive enough to stick around to see how this thing would turn out, and then she took that song from zero to one hundred in about one second.

The fact that Selena would sing my demo with the same kind of heart and talent she put into singing any song our band did meant a lot to me. That recording was a source of comfort to me for a long time after Selena was murdered, because it was something of hers that I could hold on to as my very own.

For our second wedding anniversary, I decided that the gift Selena needed more than anything else was a romantic getaway—a retreat from music, the fashion boutiques, housework, and even the dogs. I wanted to take her somewhere beautiful, a place we had never been to before, a location far enough from her family and work that

Selena and I could just be together and completely relax. We'd taken that trip to Acapulco at the start of our relationship, of course, but even that had been in the company of her brother and sister. This was going to be our trip alone.

After talking to a few people, I decided on Ocho Rios, Jamaica. This was the first time I had ever planned a trip on such a grand scale, so I had a travel agent help me choose the resort and make the arrangements. I then hid the package with the tickets and brochures in my bedside table underneath some other reading materials, praying that Selena wouldn't look there.

I had expected to meet some resistance from Selena's family. To my surprise, though, when I told them the plan, even Abraham didn't say anything negative. They kept my secret, too, so Selena was shocked when we arrived in the San Antonio airport after a concert and I told her we weren't going home with the rest of the family because we had a connecting flight to Miami.

Selena was all excited, thinking that Miami would be our final destination. She loved to shop in Miami. All I had told her in advance was that she was going to need a bathing suit because we were going somewhere tropical.

I can't remember now what it was, but Selena said something to me as we were boarding the flight to Miami that made me say, "What are you talking about? You don't do that in Jamaica!"

Selena started jumping up and down and laughing. "I got you to tell me! I got you to tell me!" she teased.

"Just for that little trick, maybe I ought to take you home," I said.

"No, come on, tell me, are we really going to Jamaica? All by ourselves?" she said.

"We are," I told her, and she put her arms around me.

I might have felt worse about Selena guessing our destination, except that I had another surprise for her as well: a ring that I'd had made by a jeweler friend back in San Antonio. It was just a simple white gold band, but I'd had the jeweler add a row of small diamonds. I was sure that Selena would love that bit of flash combined with the ring's simple elegance.

Once we landed in Jamaica, I started having doubts about my choice, because outside the airport shuttle windows the scenery looked so much like many of the smaller towns in Mexico we'd already visited. It was dark because there were no streetlights, and I was growing increasingly nervous—how much could I trust that travel agent, really?—but Selena was still having a great time, chattering away and fully enjoying herself.

I wasn't going to ruin the moment for her. Besides, the farther we got from the airport, the more aware I was of the fact that we were finally alone.

All of a sudden, the airport shuttle started slowing down. I heard the strains of a reggae band through the open windows, so I thought that we must be getting closer to the resort. Then I saw a single light with a bunch of people beneath it.

"What's going on?" Selena asked. "It looks like a party. Those people are all dancing."

Sure enough, we were still in the middle of nowhere, but these Jamaicans were having a blast beneath the single streetlight of their small town, dancing to reggae music issuing from one big speaker and drinking Red Stripe beer out of brown bottles. They were having such a good time that Selena couldn't resist standing up right in the middle of the shuttle bus and dancing.

"Sit down!" I told her as the bus lurched over yet another pothole in the road. "I don't want you to get hurt before we even get to the resort!"

The bus turned onto another road, a long driveway, and then suddenly we were at the resort. Everything was brightly lit and looked beautiful. I relaxed completely then, knowing that I'd picked a good place for us after all.

"I can't wait to check things out," Selena said.

"Okay. Here you go." I started pulling out the brochures I'd brought with me then, and laying them on the bed.

Selena said, "Oh, man, look at this!" and "Wow, they've got this, too!" as she read about everything from horseback riding on the beach to rafting river rapids nearby. "This is paradise!"

I was laughing, but I was also thinking about how to give Selena the special ring I'd bought her for an anniversary gift. Finally I hit upon the perfect surprise. Whenever Selena went to sleep, she had this funny little habit of sometimes tucking her hand inside her pillowcase. So, while she was in the bathroom cleaning up after the trip, I slipped the ring in its little blue box into one of the pillowcases on the right side—the side Selena always slept on.

I thought that Selena would want to chill out in the room and take a nap; that way she'd find the ring immediately. Instead, she wanted to go exploring right away because she was so excited. We had a little argument about it.

"Really?" I said. "You want to do all that stuff right now, without resting first?" I tried not to stare too hard at the lump in the pillowcase.

"Yeah, I really want to see everything," she said.

Finally I said, "Okay, whatever you want to do," because of course the last thing I wanted was to ruin our special trip.

We went out, and had dinner and some drinks. Then we walked around the resort and checked out the beach at night. It was a clear night and we had a good view of the moon and the stars. We had such a good time that I completely forgot about the ring as we walked on the beach under the moonlight, where we started to talk again about starting a family.

"I can't believe you did this for me," Selena said. "Things are so perfect. Nobody has ever been as good to me as you are, Chris."

That's when it hit me, bam! I'd left the ring in the pillowcase! Now I started to sweat, sure that the maids had come in and tidied up the room while we were out, and worrying that the ring might have been stolen.

I started acting like I was really tired. "Yeah, it's been a great night, and this is a beautiful spot," I said with a big yawn. "I'm glad you like it. Let's go on back to the room and rest, okay? Tomorrow we can try those river rapids or whatever you want to do."

We started walking back to the room then, with me trying not to break into a run. To my relief, I could see that the ring was still there.

Sure enough, that night Selena lay on the right side of the bed like she always did. I sat up and turned the TV on, which Selena never minded as she was going to sleep.

All of a sudden, I heard her say, "Huh? What's this?" as she reached her hand into the pillowcase.

"What's what?" I said, grinning down at her beautiful face.

Selena pulled the ring box out and opened it. She jumped out of bed and put the ring on, her lip trembling a little. "Oh, Chris," she said. "You didn't."

"I did," I said. "Happy anniversary."

She started crying then, really sobbing. She climbed back into bed with me and I held her until she was smiling again. We fell asleep that way, wrapped in each other's arms.

That trip to Jamaica only confirmed what I'd always known about Selena: my wife was an adventuress. She wasn't the sort of woman who was going to just lie around the beach if she could go exploring.

We could have stayed at our all-inclusive resort and done nothing more than lounge by the pool or dip ourselves in the warm surf, but Selena was determined to make the most of our precious free time together. One of the things she had never tried was riding river rapids, so off we went on a tour that included not only shooting the rapids on a wild green river, but also hiking and climbing up steep rocky trails. Selena was physically fit—not from going to the gym, but because she was always dancing—so she had no trouble on those climbs. I just made sure that I was the one behind her while she climbed them in her bikini!

At one point, we were given the option of taking a shuttle bus home from whatever remote place in the jungle we were, but Selena and I chose to extend our excursion. We rented a boat, almost like a canoe, and paddled upriver. It was as if we were the only people in a new world, surrounded as we were by tropical plants, insects, and animals we'd never seen before. There were even monkeys in the trees.

It was our own special Eden, and whenever things got hectic for us after that—as they were destined to be, given Selena's rapid rise to fame—I would remember the dreamy look on Selena's face in our private paradise.

TWELVE

AMOR PROHIBIDO

Courtesy of Everett Collection

*T*he band was conducting a sound check with Selena on-stage when one of her biggest hits of all time was born.

We were fiddling with the equipment and tuning our instruments when Selena just started spontaneously singing the words to "Bidi Bidi Bom Bom." I had never seen these lyrics lying around the house, despite the fact that Selena was always writing in notebooks and on little scraps of paper and leaving them wherever she happened to be sitting or standing when she got an idea for a song.

To this day, I can't remember what stage we were on when we created "Bidi Bidi Bom Bom" together. Many of the events during 1993 and 1994 are a blur because we were keeping up such a frantic professional pace. Selena y Los Dinos had been riding high since winning the Grammy for *Selena Live!* Ever since the concert at the Memorial Coliseum in Corpus Christi, Texas, we had been performing constantly, hitting both our usual venues and commanding many larger ones.

More than twenty thousand people turned out to hear us at the Pasadena Fairgrounds in August 1993, for instance, and in September we drew a crowd of seventy thousand at La Feria de Nuevo Leon in Mexico. That October, Selena was one of the featured performers at the Tejano Grand Finale show of the Coca-Cola Road Trip at Guadalupe Plaza Park in Houston.

At the Houston Livestock Show and Rodeo in February 1994, we pulled in over sixty thousand people. What's more, to commemorate Selena's five years as a company representative, Coca-Cola put out a special "Selena" Coke bottle, a collector's edition that sold out almost as soon as it appeared on the shelves.

We were all amazed at the pace of our success. Like Selena, we were humbled by it as well. The band members tried to just focus on doing what we did best: play music together. Truthfully, because of the lights, we couldn't usually see past the first few rows of people when we were onstage anyway. Here we'd be on this little stage that felt disconnected from the world, until we heard and felt all of this great energy from our fans that we'd feed right back into our music.

The night that Selena started singing the lyrics to "Bidi Bidi Bom Bom" was one of those great nights in 1994. The words "*bidi bidi bom bom*" are meant to be the sound of a beating heart, and this song tells the story of someone so entranced by her crush that her heart goes crazy and starts pounding whenever he walks by. As Selena tried out her lyrics, I started playing a guitar riff to accompany her, just having some fun. She grinned at me and kept singing.

"Stop!" A.B. called to me from the other side of the stage. "What key are you in?"

"B flat," I said.

"What are your chords?" he asked.

I told him and played a little turnaround. A.B. came up with a bass line and we started playing together. Suzette started a rhythm pattern on the drums and the song just kind of happened right there onstage.

Then the show began, and Selena was enjoying herself onstage as she always did. To be a truly successful entertainer, you have to be doing something onstage that makes people stop and stare. Selena always came out dancing. Beyond that, she communicated directly with her audience in ways that many entertainers don't know how; these days, especially, entertainers stick to their scripts. Selena wasn't like that.

No matter how successful we became, every one of our shows was different, because Selena always stayed in the moment. If she'd heard a funny joke before coming onstage, she would tell that joke in between songs. She was always real, and people could pick up on the fact that this wasn't an act. Selena never made people feel like they were watching a show. She recognized that the people in the audience were just like her, and made everyone feel as if we were all enjoying the evening together. That's a hard thing to do when you're up onstage, but Selena pulled it off every time.

The band never did anything by rote, either. We would always change up the set list, because A.B. would watch the crowd closely to see what kind of music they were reacting to and call out the songs accordingly. Other than the first song, we never had any idea what we'd be playing on a given night or in what order. We would just go.

On this particular night, Selena was talking to the crowd between songs when I heard A.B. call out, "Hey, let's play that song you were doing in sound check, Selena." He started playing the rhythm pattern and Suzette jumped in. I came in with the guitar intro and Selena started singing the words. Obviously she had written them somewhere or had them in her head. The crowd went nuts for it.

Afterward, A.B. was all smiles. "That's going to be our new hit song," he announced.

Back in the studio, Selena worked with Pete to put the lyrics and the melody together, and we recorded "Bidi Bidi Bom Bom" as one of the tracks on the new album we were working on, *Amor Prohibido*. When it came time to add my part, A.B. told me how we were going to arrange the song and then said, "Here's where you'll do your guitar solo."

Then he left the studio, trusting me to put together a solo that would work. I remember thinking, *This song is going to be huge*, because I felt it the way A.B. did. "Bidi Bidi Bom Bom" was a woman's proud celebration of love. I wanted to create a radical guitar solo that would truly blend a hard rock sound into a Tejano cumbia, in much the same way that Selena and I had grown up in traditional families to become a contemporary couple. I wanted, more than anything, to support the rich, optimistic sound of Selena's singing with my guitar.

The song worked on every level, and before long, "Bidi Bidi Bom Bom" took on a life of its own, becoming one of Selena's most beloved, most enduring hits.

I don't know how that song just fell into place like that. I don't even know how we managed to find time to make the next album. The more successful Selena became, the more we had to travel and the more pressure she felt. To add to her time constraints, both of the boutiques were now off the ground in Corpus Christi and San Antonio, and she was traveling to Monterrey with increasing frequency to talk about opening a clothing factory and a boutique there. If Abraham, Suzette, her mom, or I couldn't accompany her somewhere, Selena sometimes asked Yolanda to go with her.

We were still playing a lot of concerts in Mexico, and we had also started performing in other Latin American countries. We were always treated like celebrities—more so than in the U.S.—and given luxurious accommodations.

In one hotel in El Salvador, for instance, I was standing by myself in the lobby when I suddenly realized that I was surrounded not only by the usual El Salvadoran armed militia men, walking around in their army gear and carrying machine guns, but also by the U.S. Secret Service.

I scanned the lobby to figure out the reason for all of the security, knowing it couldn't possibly be us. I was startled to see former President George Bush and his wife Barbara standing not quite five feet away from me. I edged away from them slowly, trying not to look suspicious, afraid that somehow I'd make a wrong move and be shot on the spot.

Another time, Selena and I were playing a show in Monterrey when I saw billboards advertising the appearance of the Scorpions, a popular heavy metal band that I had admired since childhood. I had always wanted to see them play live, and as we returned to the hotel after our show, I was feeling a little down that I hadn't known in advance that they were playing in Mexico, too.

As Selena and I stepped into the hotel elevator with our security guard, a couple of other people were already there. One man was small in stature, maybe just five feet tall, and wearing a black beret.

When he and the other man didn't move out of the way, Selena and I had to slip into the elevator behind them.

Just as the elevator started moving, the smaller man in front of me turned to say something to his companion, and I realized that he was Klaus Meine, the legendary lead singer of the Scorpions. I elbowed Selena in the side.

"What?" she said loudly.

I felt my face go hot. I didn't want the singer to know that I'd spotted him. "Nothing, never mind," I said. "It's no big deal."

Inside, though, I was going crazy. Selena was still staring at me, so I jerked my head at the guy in front of us again and silently mouthed, "It's him! It's Klaus Meine!"

Selena mouthed back, "Huh? What?"

Finally the Scorpions got off on their floor. As soon as the elevator door closed, I started freaking out. "That was him!" I said. "That was Klaus, the lead singer from the Scorpions!"

"What? And you didn't say hi?" Selena cried.

"No, no. I didn't want to bother him." I dug my hands into my pockets.

"You want to go down and find him?" she said. "Let's go get his autograph!"

"No, that's all right," I insisted. "He's one of the biggest stars in Mexico! I'm not going to go chasing him for an autograph."

"I can't believe you," she said. "Why not?"

"Because I'm not as brave as you," I said, and that made her laugh.

During another tour in Mexico, Selena y Los Dinos played a big concert with a lot of other popular Latin American artists. One of them was Alejandra Guzman, known as the "Queen of Rock" in

Latin America. I remember the first time I ever saw Alejandra and heard her sing. This was on Big Bertha, right after I'd joined Los Dinos and long before Selena and I were a couple. The TV was on, and Alejandra was performing on one of those Spanish-language variety shows.

"Man, who's that?" I asked Selena as we sat there watching Alejandra sing.

Selena told me Alejandra's name and laughed. "Why, do you like her?"

"Sure, she's hot," I said, just to tease Selena. "Let me check this out."

In fact, it was Alejandra's music that I admired more than anything else. I went through a serious Alejandra phase after that, buying her CDs and listening to her music.

So, naturally, when Alejandra came into the back dressing room to meet us during that show in Mexico, she and Selena started joking around, and Selena said in Spanish, "Hey, Alejandra, come and meet my husband Chris. He has a huge crush on you."

I wanted to protest, but of course my Spanish wasn't good enough, and Selena and Alejandra were already cracking up at my flustered expression anyway. I knew it was a lost cause.

Selena and I respected each other as artists. I knew how great she was: Selena had the talent, voice, personality, and looks to make it to the top. For her part, Selena admired how different I was from other Tejano musicians. The other guys in our band were really good at Tejano music and I learned a lot from them, but by 1994 I was adding my licks on top, bringing their best stuff along for the ride with me and adding a legitimate rock sound to Los Dinos, as I had with our remix of "Fotos y Recuerdos," a song originally done by the Pretenders, on *Amor Prohibido*.

I don't remember Selena ever playing the diva. She never complained about her mix or the sound onstage, which is rare for most vocalists. I never heard her say, "I don't want to do that." She was talented enough that she could stop by the studio while the band was working on a new song, hum her part a little, and then go off to shop at the mall, saying, "Don't worry about me. I'll know what to do when y'all are ready to record this."

We didn't have to worry. To be perfectly honest, I never heard Selena do anything wrong onstage. None of us ever had to ask her to change something in the studio, either. In fact, sometimes she'd track her vocals by herself, and she would be the one who would request a second take so that she could add little harmonies she'd create on her own. She was that good, and she was getting better with every album.

For *Amor Prohibido*, we did things the way we always did. Like a well-oiled machine, Selena and the band members laid down our tracks separately in the studio only after we'd perfected them during preproduction sessions, and then A.B. arranged and mixed the music. There was one exception to this. Late the night before we were supposed to go into the studio, I got a phone call from A.B.

"Can you come over and listen to something real quick?" he asked.

I went to his house and listened to "Ya No," which would become the last song on the CD. It was a *conjunto* song with an accordion. "I want to turn this into a rock song," A.B. said after I'd heard it a couple of times. "What do you think? Can you do it?"

"What, you mean for the album?" I asked. "But aren't we supposed to be in the studio first thing tomorrow morning?"

He nodded. "What do you think?"

"Okay," I said. "I'll try."

We spent the night in his studio, trying to get an arrangement done that worked. Selena was at home, calling repeatedly as we worked. "Is he okay?" she asked A.B. "You all are still there?"

Finally she fell asleep. When we were finished, I walked from A.B.'s house to ours feeling just dead tired and wondering how I was going to get up in the morning, drive to San Antonio, and record this album.

When we woke up the next morning, Selena said, "So how did it go?"

"It went," I said. "But I don't know how it's going to sound today."

"You're going to be okay," she reassured me. "I can't wait to hear it."

We went into San Antonio and recorded the instrumentals for *Amor Prohibido*. Then Selena went in separately to record her vocal tracks. When I heard it all put together, I remember thinking how incredibly mature Selena's voice sounded. There was a noticeable difference between her voice on this album and *Entre a Mi Mundo*, especially.

I can't say it was an improvement, exactly, because I always thought that Selena's voice sounded incredible. It's just that her voice was richer and more mature than before, and her singing was more emotional and powerful as a result.

"The fans aren't ready for this one, Selena," I told her.

"What do you mean?" she asked.

"This is a different kind of album, in a good way," I said. "You sound incredible, and A.B. is right. This is going to be a major hit."

It was. Songs from *Amor Prohibido* were all over the radio as soon as the album was released. The title track catapulted to number one on *Billboard*'s Latin chart to become the biggest hit yet in Selena's career. That song, along with "No Me Queda Mas," became the most successful singles of 1994 and 1995 in both the U.S. Latino communities and Mexico.

Amor Prohibido went on to win Album of the Year at the 1995 Tejano Music Awards in January, where Selena was awarded top honors in six of the fifteen categories, including Female Vocalist for an unprecedented seventh year in a row and Female Entertainer of the Year. "Bidi Bidi Bom Bom" won as Song of the Year.

We were truly on a fast train now, and there seemed to be nothing but more success in our future. Every now and then, though, I'd look at my gorgeous, talented wife, and wish that I could take her back to Jamaica, where we could be alone again on the beach by the light of the moon.

It was during this frenzied time in 1994 that Selena and I hit the only truly rough patch in our marriage. Like most young couples, I suppose, we were making the adjustment from the novelty of living together to the reality of handling the pressures of daily life long term. In our case, the pressures were more extreme, perhaps, because of our intense work and travel schedules—Selena's, especially.

Because Selena now had Yolanda to accompany her on trips, I sometimes was able to stay home, as I did when Selena had to fly to Los Angeles to make the music video for "Bidi Bidi Bom Bom," or when Selena and Yolanda had business to conduct for the boutiques. Selena wasn't so lucky. She never, ever caught a break.

At times, everyone in the band was so tired that we had to operate on autopilot just to get through our days. The music video for "No Me Queda Mas" was filmed in San Antonio, thankfully, so nobody had to travel far. The band shots were of us playing inside the train station, where Selena sang on a stairway wearing a white dress. She had also done a full day of shooting the day before on the Riverwalk, however, so she was beat.

After we completed the video shoot at the train station, we all had to drive home to Corpus. Abraham had the tour bus there. I could have stayed at my mom's, but the lure of my own bed in Corpus made me decide to drive my truck back behind the bus.

"You go on ahead on the bus and get some rest in your bunk," I told Selena, because she looked so drained. "You don't have to ride in the truck with me."

"Really?" she said. "You sure?"

"Yeah, I'll be fine. I've got the radio."

"Thank you, Chris," she said with a sigh, and kissed me good night.

All the way home, I followed the bus on the highway and imagined Selena crashed on her bunk, her hand tucked into the pillowcase. I'd never been more exhausted in my life. A part of me wished right then for simpler times.

That kind of travel exhaustion led to the worst fights of our marriage. Selena liked to just go into the house and go back to sleep whenever the tour bus dropped us off after a show, leaving me to do whatever was necessary to wrestle our luggage into the house and check on the animals.

One night, coming home from a tour, we were both in a bad mood. Selena liked to be awakened gently, but on this particular occasion, I was out of patience with everything and everybody, so I just shook her shoulder and said, "Hey. It's time to get off the bus."

Selena woke up angry. She got to her feet and said, "Get out of my way, Chris. I'm going inside."

I was trying to retrieve something out of the bunk across from hers. Selena came down the aisle fast, no doubt focused on getting into the house and crawling into bed, and barreled right into me.

"Hey, what's wrong with you?" I demanded, stubbornly blocking her path. "You almost knocked me over! Just wait a minute and let me get my stuff."

"No," she said. "I want to go in now." Selena pushed me aside and stomped toward the door leading to the front lounge area of the bus.

I thought her tantrum was funny and started to laugh. Big mistake. That pushed Selena's buttons and made her even angrier than before. She turned around and came at me again, intent on pushing me or something, just as the bus driver was walking up the steps.

Just as Selena reached me, I turned sideways and she completely missed. She lost her balance and fell down in the aisle.

The bus driver took one look at what was going on, turned around, and walked off the bus. I helped Selena up, shaking my head. "Great," I said. "I hope you're happy. Now the driver thinks I'm abusing you or something."

Selena just shrugged me off and went inside.

I don't get angry easily, but my nerves were already frayed from performing and traveling, I really lost my temper at that point. I started yanking our luggage off the bus as fast as I could, fuming about how unfair it was that Selena always got to just go inside and crash after a trip, while she took it for granted that it was my job to unload the gear and take care of everything else. She wasn't a diva with her fans. Why was she acting this way with me?

I had just gotten this beautiful two-thousand-dollar guitar and it was in a gig bag; it was the last thing I brought inside to the house. I set it on the sofa and then went into the bedroom and put something of Selena's on the bed. Then I went back into the living room to get my guitar.

All of a sudden, I heard a crash from the bedroom. I knew right away what Selena had done: she had kicked her stuff off the bed. I rolled my eyes and thought, *Oh, really? She's going to be that way?*

I got my guitar and came back into the bedroom. I set the guitar on the bed, not anywhere near her, and went back out to the living room to retrieve one more bag. I heard another "boom" and thought, *No way was that my guitar!*

When I rushed back into the bedroom, I saw that Selena had, indeed, thrashed out with her legs and kicked my guitar right off the bed and onto the floor—something that she would have had to really go out of her way to do, since I'd put the guitar on the opposite side of the bed.

I went into a rage. "What is wrong with you?" I shouted.

Selena sat up in bed and we started yelling at each other like a couple of toddlers. "You pushed me on the bus!" she shouted.

"I did not! You were coming after me!" I argued. "You know that's the truth. All I did was sidestep when you were attacking me!"

Looking back on this moment now, I know that it was just two people in a bad mood. Yet the argument escalated until I got so angry that I told her, "You want to start kicking shit around with me? Fine, then. Here!"

I grabbed my guitar up off the floor and hurled it right over her legs and into a table across the room. It knocked the table down and broke several things that had been on top, but I didn't care.

"I'm sick of this, and I don't need this hassle! I'm tired of it!" I shouted. Then I turned around and walked out of the room.

I made it as far as the living room. I was seriously prepared to walk out of that house. I had never been so upset with my wife. How dared she treat me like I was always going to be her servant?

I was just about to open the door when Selena came up behind me and grabbed my arm. She was crying. "I'm sorry. Don't leave," she begged. "I didn't mean to act that way!"

"Then why did you?" I said, giving her a hug. "I don't mean to act like that either. It's just that there's only so much I can take. I have to unload all of my stuff and yours, too, every time, while all you have to do is get off the bus and come inside. I don't mind doing that, but you have to realize that I'm tired, too."

We made up, then, and things were fine. Much later, after Yolanda had shot and killed my wife, she would say to the press that our marriage was on the rocks and that Selena had been prepared to divorce me. She concocted some story—one of many lies that Yolanda told over time—about how I had even punched a door and then pulled it right off its hinges.

It is true that Selena and I sometimes argued, but I don't think that she and I ever experienced anything out of the ordinary. Most couples whose marriages last reach some point in their lives together—or maybe many points, if the marriage is long enough—

where they have to decide that they're still committed enough to stay in the relationship.

During this rough patch of ours, a friend of mine said, "Man, you can't break up with Selena! She's like the ultimate rich and beautiful trophy wife!"

"That's not how I see it," I told him. But then I stopped talking about it with him, because I was at a loss for words.

How could I possibly explain that, even though I admired the talented person Selena was onstage and her voice went straight to my heart, that's not why I was in love with her? I loved the real Selena, the silly Selena with the contagious laugh and her love of dogs and kids, the woman who wrapped a bandanna around her hair while she cleaned the house, the daredevil who rode my motorcycle with me at night around the bay. I loved my wife.

Yet, in the worst stress of trying to manage our performing schedule, the house, and Selena's new business, there was a brief time when both Selena and I had thoughts about whether we should just move on. We weren't really arguing at that point; it was more like things had just stopped clicking.

Both of us had reached a point in our relationship—and in our lives—when we were feeling disconnected emotionally, and asking ourselves whether we wanted to do something else. I didn't want to cling to her.

I think that, had I been as old then as I am now, I might have felt differently and worked harder. As it was, though, I didn't feel I should stand in the way if Selena wanted to live on her own for a while.

During this whole rough patch, which didn't last more than a few weeks, we danced around the idea of separating, even while we were still thrown together all of the time because of our performances. At one point, Selena and I were seated next to each other on an airplane talking about trying life apart for a while.

"Look, if this is what you need, you know that I'm not going to stand in your way, but it's not my first choice," I said.

"Yeah, I know," she said.

Selena was serious enough about possibly separating to discuss it with A.B. He told me later that she had come to him to air her frustrations and doubts.

"Okay, then," A.B. said to her. "This is what I'm going to ask you, and it's the only thing I'm going to ask you. How would you feel if you decided to separate or get a divorce or whatever, and then you saw Chris walking around with some other woman?"

"Oh, no, that's not going to happen!" Selena answered.

Shortly after that conversation with her brother, everything came back around. To Selena, I said, "I don't want to keep fighting like this. I love you. But if I can't make you happy, you deserve to go find your way and be happy with someone else."

She started crying. "I don't want to be happy with anyone else," she said. "I just want to be happy with you."

I pulled her close. "Then let's be happy together," I whispered into her hair. "We can do it. I know we can."

The odd thing was that, after that one short, rough patch, everything between us was even better than before. It was as if we were newlyweds again, loving each other and finding our way together in the world as a team.

We decided that it was time to take the next step in our relationship and move away from her parents. We wanted to buy land and build a house of our own, so that we could be ready when it was time to start a family. Selena was still talking about five kids. Even crazier than that were the names she wanted to give those children of ours: long, fancy names like "Sebastian."

"That's crazy. Think about what a tough time our kids would have in kindergarten, trying to spell their own names," I teased. "I think we should just give our sons regular-sounding names, maybe like 'Eric' or something."

One thing we definitely agreed on, though, was that we wanted to buy a big piece of property that was still close to central Corpus Christi. There weren't many properties that fit that bill, so it didn't take us long to look.

Fortunately, after seeing just a couple of tracts of land, we found the property that spoke to us. "This is it," Selena declared, the minute we stepped out of my truck and started following the Realtor around to see the property lines.

It was ten acres, with a hill that would be the perfect site for the house that we planned to fill with the sounds of music, children, and laughter. There was a pond for our children to fish in, and a creek where we could wade or just dream in the shade. Selena could have her horses, finally. Those ten acres were custom made for us, and we placed an offer on that land the same day we saw it.

"I can really see us here," I said. "When I'm, like, eighty years old, I'm going to sit right here on the porch of our house. I'll be so bored that I'll spend the afternoons cracking pecans with a pair of pliers, and we'll have so much time on our hands that there will be hundreds of coffee cans full of shelled pecans all over the damn porch."

Selena laughed. "And what will I be doing, if the kids are gone and I'm not singing anymore?"

I looked her over, keeping a straight face. "You? You'll be sitting right here on the porch next to me, knitting."

Our love had been renewed because Selena and I had truly examined what we had discovered in each other—and how much we stood to lose if we parted. Now we were ready to accompany each other into a future filled with love and family. We had found a place to build our home and grow old together.

We might never make it back to Jamaica, but this would be our own retreat, a private piece of paradise just for Selena and me. It was perfect.

THIRTEEN

THE DAY THE WORLD STOPPED

AP Photo / *Houston Chronicle, John Everett*

*W*hat we didn't know, of course, was that the cancer was growing while we went on with our lives. Yolanda seemed to be everywhere now, determined not to just have a finger in every pie, but her whole hand. She had become so involved in running the boutiques that Selena had given her complete access to all checking and credit card accounts.

Honestly, it was probably Martin Gomez, the fashion designer working closely with Selena on her clothing designs, who first started noticing something off with Yolanda. He would bring little things to Selena's attention, examples of how Yolanda was manipulating people or trying to control too many aspects of the business.

Martin told us that some of the other employees in the boutiques were having run-ins with Yolanda and were threatening to quit. "She's mean and controlling," he told Selena. "There's a lot of tension at work. She yells at my seamstresses and even at me. I don't think I can work under these conditions."

It was true that when Selena first started the boutiques, she had friends working for her. Yolanda had slowly gotten rid of Selena's friends. Now, according to Martin, Yolanda had also started telling people that they shouldn't call Selena directly anymore—they should call her instead. She was acting more like Selena's bodyguard than a personal assistant. When one of Martin's seamstresses went to Yolanda's house to pick something up, she had been startled to discover that the walls were covered with Selena's photos.

"I just think it's kind of weird how Yolanda is trying to get in between you and everybody else," Martin told Selena. "She's obsessed with you and I'm a little scared of her."

Martin's concerns should have been a red flag for us. As always, though, Selena and I were so busy that we overlooked all of the signs showing us that Yolanda was truly becoming unhinged. Truthfully, Martin was opinionated, like most artists, and we figured that like most artists he didn't want anyone telling him what to do. When it came to Yolanda and Martin and their conflicts, we really didn't think there was anything going on beyond a couple of people having too much attitude and going at each other.

Selena, meanwhile, still trusted Yolanda. In fact, she was glad to have Yolanda take calls and otherwise run interference for her at the boutiques. She even gave Yolanda a key to our house.

In addition to keeping up with her intense performance schedule, Selena was becoming more and more determined to get her clothing factory and boutique up and running in Mexico, and Yolanda was helping her. Since Yolanda was fluent in Spanish, she would go into business meetings in Mexico with Selena—something I would have been useless at, since I neither spoke Spanish fluently nor had much knowledge about the fashion industry.

Gradually, though, even Selena and I started noticing that Yolanda was becoming clingier and odder. Whenever Selena was in San Antonio, Yolanda would try to insist on going everywhere with her. Or Yolanda would call Selena at odd hours and tell her, "We have to go to Monterrey, because so-and-so wants us to have a meeting. We have to go right now!" Then she would get irritated because Selena wouldn't jump when she said "jump."

Selena, though, was loyal—especially to anyone in her close circle of family and friends. She tried to shield Yolanda for a long time. When Martin said that certain employees were complaining about Yolanda, Selena responded, "Those people are probably only complaining because Yolanda is the boss and they don't want to listen to her."

Besides, Yolanda always did everything in her power to make what seemed like her undying devotion to Selena abundantly clear—especially when she gave Selena a ring shaped like the Fabergé eggs Selena collected.

She had gotten her first one a couple of years earlier on one of our trips to Miami. We were staying in the Intercontinental Hotel there and, as always, Selena insisted on going into the gift shop. There, she saw her first Fabergé egg—an ostrich egg encrusted in gold with different precious stones set into it.

"It's so beautiful," she said.

For some reason, Selena was fascinated by that egg, so I bought it for her. She loved it, and from then on, I continued to buy Fabergé eggs for her whenever I saw them. I think that she was intrigued because, to her, eggs represented the beginning of life. The Fabergé eggs were also incredible handcrafted works of art. Selena's egg collection became her pride and joy. She eventually started displaying the collection in our house, in glass-fronted cabinets—probably thirty or forty eggs in all.

Yolanda knew this, of course, so when some of the staff members at the boutiques wanted to pool their money to buy Selena a gift, she told them to give the money to her and she would have a ring made that she knew Selena would love. The ring was beautiful—a gold ring with a white-gold egg set on top of it. Fifty-two tiny, glittering diamonds were embedded in the egg; on the fourteen-karat band itself, the letter "S" was engraved three times.

"I bought this for you," Yolanda said, never mentioning how she had asked the other coworkers to contribute to the gift, or the fact that she had charged the $3,000 price for it on Selena's corporate American Express account.

Selena was thrilled with the gift and started wearing it right away. "Look, Chris," she said when she showed it to me. "See how thoughtful Yolanda can be?"

Why didn't we detect the cancer? We were oblivious partly because we were even busier than ever. Our shows included playing for twenty thousand fans at Six Flags AstroWorld's Southern Star Amphitheater in July, and performing with Mazz and Emilio Navaira in the third annual Tejano Superfest.

In December 1994, Selena headlined the New Year's Eve dance at the George R. Brown Convention Center, and in January, she played a concert at the Houston Livestock Show and Rodeo in the Houston Astrodome for over sixty-five thousand fans. She was the headliner at Miami's Calle Ocho Festival as well, which drew over one hundred thousand music lovers. Our album *Amor Prohibido* was nominated for a Grammy in 1994, and Selena recorded a duet called "Donde Quiera Que Estes" with the Barrio Boyz that hit number one on *Billboard*'s Hot Latin Tracks.

New opportunities for Selena continued to open up. In early 1995, she began making plans to create a perfume line. She was also excited to be given opportunities to explore acting. She really wanted to try being an actress and, as we had all discovered through making music videos and television commercials, she was good at it, too—a natural in front of the camera.

One of our promoters arranged for Selena to make guest appearances on *Dos Mujeres, Un Camino,* a popular Latin American soap opera, to give her exposure to an even broader audience. Selena was excited by the chance to appear on TV, but she was disappointed by that particular experience. She didn't really enjoy playing the character as it was written for her, especially when the director told her that she had to kiss an actor playing a musician in a band.

"I'm not going to do that," she protested. "I'm married. I just can't. It's not right."

A friend of mine later asked if Selena had refused to kiss the other actor because of me, but I knew that wasn't it. I was not insecure with her in any way. Maybe that's another thing she saw in me: the fact that I wasn't ever going to be one of those possessive men who was out to control her. People made comments about her body all of the time, but I never reacted to them, because I knew those rude remarks came with the celebrity turf.

If Selena had decided that she needed to kiss another actor to play her role convincingly, I would have been supportive. One thing that did bug me, though, was a Mexican tabloid that came out during Selena's soap opera stint; the tabloid ran an interview with the guy who played Selena's main love interest in the soap opera. The interviewer asked him the usual stupid questions, including, "If you could be with anybody one night, who would you pick?"

"Selena," the actor answered.

But I wasn't worried about Selena, simply because of how she was. Selena wasn't in any way a flirt. She didn't use sexuality to get what she wanted. She used her brains and her talent to achieve her goals. That other stuff just happened to come along with her when she was onstage. She was comfortable in her own skin, so she didn't have to put on that kind of act so many celebrities do, where they walk into a room and expect everyone to turn around and stare in awe. Selena was always too down-to-earth to behave like a movie star.

Selena's second acting experience was much more fun than the first. She was asked to play a small part as a mariachi singer in a movie called *Don Juan DeMarco*, starring Faye Dunaway, Johnny Depp, and Marlon Brando. We were both really excited about this, not only because it was an opportunity for Selena to be seen by many moviegoers who probably had never listened to Tejano music in their lives, but because of the high caliber of the actors involved.

We flew to Los Angeles, where the scene was filmed in the Biltmore Hotel, and when we arrived, Selena was really cool and calm. I was the one freaking out.

When it was her call time, we walked downstairs to the lobby of the Biltmore. Johnny Depp was there, and he came right over and introduced himself. Selena was still collected and poised, completely unfazed. She went off to do her scene—over and over again—and I finally went back to the room because the filming took so long.

Selena eventually came back upstairs, exhausted but happy. "Man, that Marlon Brando, he sure likes to flirt," she said.

Shortly after Yolanda gave Selena the ring, things started going from bad to worse in the boutiques. Our paperwork wasn't matching up and money was missing. There were charges on our credit cards that weren't accounted for. Selena noticed these financial discrepancies because she was the one who went over her business accounts and the bills.

Selena hired her cousin Debra to work in the boutiques and help expand the business into Mexico. Debra quit within a week, telling Yolanda that she was unhappy with how staff members weren't reporting their sales. Yolanda told Selena not to worry about any of this. "I'll take care of the problem," Yolanda promised.

Soon after that, Martin Gomez asked Selena to buy him out of his contract, because he felt that he could no longer work with Yolanda. "She's been mismanaging affairs from the start," he said, and told Selena that Yolanda had destroyed some of his original designs and hadn't paid his bills.

Both stores began to suffer losses. Yolanda fired anyone she didn't like, so employee attrition was steady; the staff had been cut in half and employees continued to complain about the way Yolanda treated everyone. Selena turned a deaf ear, not wanting to believe that Yolanda would ever do anything to hurt her.

Eventually, the employees started talking to Abraham, who in turn expressed his concerns about Yolanda's business management skills—or lack of them—to Selena. She tried to laugh this off as well.

"Dad always thinks people are bad," she told me. "You know he never trusts anyone."

By early March, however, Selena and I could no longer deny that there were problems in every aspect of the business that involved

Yolanda—which was most of them—and in the fan club as well. Certain people had sent in cash or checks to become fan club members, but they had never gotten the T-shirts and other items they were supposed to receive in exchange; they were now writing or calling to complain. Yolanda was even instructing some fans to make checks directly out to her instead of to the fan club.

Abraham started to receive calls from some of Selena's disappointed, confused fans. On March 9, he called Yolanda into the offices at Q Productions for a private meeting along with Selena and Suzette to find out what was going on.

Yolanda couldn't explain herself, Selena told me later. As Abraham questioned her, Yolanda kept repeating, "I don't know, I don't know."

Abraham told Yolanda to get off their property and to never step foot on it again, or he'd have her arrested. He also threatened to take her to court for embezzlement.

Suzette called Yolanda a thief and a liar, and said that she was disgusted that a woman she had trusted enough to have her participate in her wedding had been doing this to the family—and especially to Selena, who had been so good to her.

Selena was the opposite of Abraham in some ways: she was as trusting as he was suspicious. She was torn between feeling betrayed and angry as she watched Yolanda trip over her own lies, and feeling compassion toward the woman she had once considered one of her best friends.

I think that, in many ways, Selena couldn't believe what she was seeing as Yolanda unraveled right in front of us. However, by this point, she, too, was ready to sever all ties with her former friend—but first she wanted Yolanda to return the missing paperwork. The fan club had been her breaking point. To Selena, her fans were her family, and now her family had been hurt.

The morning after that meeting with Yolanda, Abraham's brother Eddie called to let Abraham know that Yolanda was at Q Productions with another employee from the Corpus Christi boutique. Abraham drove straight to the office in order to inform Yolanda again that she was no longer welcome anywhere on his property.

That same day, I heard Selena arguing with Yolanda on the phone. After Selena hung up, she said, "I can't trust her anymore."

She was right. The day after Abraham banned Yolanda from Q Productions, she went out and bought a gun.

Selena finally started quizzing various workers at the boutiques about Yolanda's behavior. They all told her that they had been having problems with Yolanda. What's more, several employees at the San Antonio salon came forward and told her that Yolanda appeared to be stealing money. Yolanda had even gotten involved in Selena's perfume line, picking up samples from Leonard Wong, the man she was working with on creating the perfume, but never giving them to Selena.

"I can't believe this is happening," Selena said to me, distressed because this had all been going unnoticed while we were busy on the road. "I should fire Yolanda, but she's still holding on to some papers we really need for our taxes. I don't want to alienate her completely and risk losing those records."

"What do you want to do?" I asked. I knew that Selena didn't want to involve Abraham. This was her business, and she wanted to resolve the problems independently from her family.

In my mind, I knew it wasn't life or death paperwork—I probably would have just let lawyers try to wrest it from Yolanda—but I also knew that it wasn't in Selena's nature to leave any stone unturned. Selena was stubborn, which is partly what made her so successful professionally; she just wanted Yolanda to return what was rightfully ours before she washed her hands of the woman whom she had once trusted so completely.

Selena and I went back and forth about possible solutions that ranged from firing Yolanda on the spot to calling in a private investigator. Finally, Selena said, "I can't let Yolanda know that we suspect her of misusing our credit cards or stealing money. I doubt that she really has any proof that she's not stealing money, like she says. But we need to get our business papers back from her for the taxes. We can't let her know that we're thinking about firing her. Not yet."

I agreed, and that's when the real game of cat-and-mouse began. Over the next two weeks, Yolanda kept claiming that she had proof that she wasn't stealing from the boutiques or embezzling money from the fan club, but every time Selena met her to see the receipts and other papers that would be evidence of Yolanda's innocence, she somehow didn't bring the right documents.

Sometime around March 15, Selena told me that she was going to meet Yolanda in a restaurant on the outskirts of Corpus to collect the necessary paperwork.

"Why can't she just bring the papers to the boutiques?" I asked.

"She's afraid," Selena said. "Yolanda won't drive into Corpus because she says she's been getting threatening phone calls."

At the restaurant, they sat in Selena's car because Yolanda was too nervous to go inside. Yolanda gave Selena almost all of the paperwork that we needed for our business—but not quite.

"Maybe I should work someplace else," Yolanda said. "This is too much for me."

I doubt very much that Yolanda really intended to resign. She was just trying to manipulate Selena. And Selena did feel sorry for Yolanda, because her former friend looked so despondent. At the same time, Selena had her own reasons for pretending to believe in Yolanda's friendship: she was still very intent on recovering our paperwork.

Thinking fast, Selena decided that the best stance to take would be a conciliatory one, at least for the time being. "No, no, no," Selena told Yolanda. "Please don't quit. I need you for the Mexico deal. I really need your help. You can't quit, not when we're so close!"

When Selena said this, Yolanda's demeanor changed completely. "She was suddenly in a good mood again, all buddy-buddy with me and laughing like we were friends," Selena told me afterward.

Then Yolanda said, "You want to see something?"

"Sure," Selena said. "What is it?"

Yolanda reached into her purse and pulled out a gun.

As Selena told me this later, I had a sinking feeling. I knew now that Yolanda was even crazier than I thought. "What the hell?" I said. "She had a gun in the car?"

"Uh-huh," Selena said, but she didn't seem at all unnerved by this. "Yolanda pulled the gun out and said she'd bought it for protection."

"What did you do?" I asked.

"I went off on her and said that she needed to take that gun back to the store right now, of course," Selena said.

Later, investigators discovered that Yolanda had gone on March 11 to a gun range and store called A Place to Shoot in San Antonio.

Yolanda had told one of the employees there that she was a private home nurse and that some family members of a patient had threatened her. She wanted the gun for protection.

Yolanda had to wait for three days for a background check, then picked up the pistol and bought twenty hollow-point bullets—the kind designed to open up fast on impact, causing maximum damage. The next day, she brought the gun when she met Selena at the restaurant.

After her meeting with Selena, Yolanda thought that they were still friends. She returned the gun to the store and told the clerk that she'd changed her mind and didn't need the pistol after all.

I still wonder sometimes if Yolanda might have shot Selena on the day she first showed her the pistol if Selena had gone ahead and dismissed her. Maybe. I carry a certain sense of guilt that I never said anything about Yolanda having shown Selena the gun in her purse.

What if I had told the police? Or Abraham? Who knows how Abraham would have reacted? Maybe he would have called in a favor with the police and had them scare Yolanda, and it would have been over. I still live with those questions.

A few weeks earlier, Selena had gone into Q Productions to work on "Dreaming of You," the song that would become the biggest hit on the mainstream English-language album we were scheduled to release later that year. I was going to go with her, but on the same day, Abraham asked me to work with the lead singer in that rock band that he was trying to promote—the one I had been working with at our house when Selena showed me how one of the songs I'd written for them should sound.

"Do you mind if I help out your dad instead of going to the studio with you?" I asked Selena.

"No, that's fine," Selena said. "You do the best you can do with this guy, and I'll be right back." She gave me a hug and a kiss. "I love you," she said.

"I love you, too," I said.

I wish that I could say that I had some kind of premonition that the end of my time with Selena was rapidly drawing near, but I did not. I just went to work. But I'll always have regrets about what happened later that day.

I worked with the singer from Abraham's rock band in our home studio right through the afternoon and into the night. I had my cell phone set to vibrate on the mixing board; I was trying to mold this singer's vocals when the cell phone went off. It was Selena.

"Hey, what are you doing?" she asked.

"Still working," I said.

"Can you get away?"

"No, I don't think so," I said.

"Please? Can't you just say you've got to go somewhere?" Selena asked. "I'd really like it if you came over to the studio."

"I could say that, but we're finally making a little progress," I hedged. "I need to see this thing through for a little bit longer. Then maybe I can come by. Why? What's so important?"

"I really want you to come hear something," Selena said. "It's that song, 'Dreaming of You.'"

I knew which song she was talking about, of course, but I hadn't yet paid much attention to the demo with the lyrics on it. I had no idea what the song was about. "I'll try," I said.

"Okay," she said. "I really want you to come over here and listen to what I did on that song."

Then we hung up. Later—much later, after it seemed like the world had ended and my heart was torn in two—I thought about that phone call. I like to imagine that Selena was thinking of me when she recorded that vocal track. I think that's the truth, too, because Selena had never before asked me to drop whatever I was doing to come hear something she was singing.

That's what I should have done—drop everything to spend a few more precious minutes with my wife. If I had done that, my last moments with Selena might have included standing right next to her in the studio and hearing that song of hers, which carries all of the feeling she had for me.

I still feel happy when I think about how Selena was thinking of me when she sang that song. But I'm also torn up by the fact that I didn't go to her then. Why didn't I just leave work so that I could listen to what my wife wanted me to hear?

The answer is simple: I didn't realize that my chances to hear Selena sing were nearly over.

On March 30, Selena and I were at home, waiting for my father to come in from out of town. He was going to spend some time with us and stay in our guest bedroom. Before my dad arrived, though, Yolanda called to say that she was at the Days Inn in Corpus and had finally brought the missing paperwork that Selena needed for her business.

"Just come over here and get the papers," Yolanda told Selena. "I don't want to have to deal with anyone."

"She sounds kind of shaky," Selena said to me after they'd hung up.

"She's always telling stories," I reminded her. "What makes you think that Yolanda has the papers this time, when she never has before?"

"I don't know, but I'm going over there," Selena said. "It's worth a shot."

"Let me drive you to the motel," I said. "I don't want you going over there at night by yourself."

I drove Selena over to the hotel in my truck and parked. Selena got out of the truck and told me that Yolanda was in Room 158.

"She wants to see me alone," Selena said. "Why don't I do that, and you stay here. She might be more likely to tell me the truth if I'm alone."

"You sure?"

"Yeah," she said. "Besides, if you're out here in the truck, I'll have a good excuse to leave."

"Okay." It was a nice night. I turned the ignition off and rolled down the windows. I listened to the radio, but when Selena didn't come back after a while, I decided I'd better go see what was going on.

I locked the truck and followed the path that Selena had taken. The door to Yolanda's room was open and light was spilling out of the doorway. I looked inside and saw that Yolanda was sitting on the bed. She looked like she had been crying. Selena was standing in front of her, looking upset as well.

"Hey," I said. "Everything okay in here?"

"Yeah, everything is cool," Selena said.

Neither of us knew that Yolanda had returned to the same gun shop in San Antonio a few days before this, where she repurchased the exact snub-nosed Taurus 45 revolver that she had bought before. I didn't see the gun. All I saw was a small, sad, ugly little woman sitting on a bed, not a murderer.

Who knows? Maybe Yolanda would have killed Selena that night, if I hadn't come along. In any case, Selena followed me back out to the truck, and told me that Yolanda had been telling her about being raped in Monterrey earlier that day.

"What?" I turned around in shock.

"Yeah, she was trying to show me her torn clothes," Selena said. "I offered to take her to the hospital, but she wouldn't go, probably because it's another one of her stories. It looks to me like Yolanda did that to herself."

We got into the truck and I started the engine. Selena turned on the overhead light and started flipping through the papers. "It's not all here," she said in frustration. "There are more papers missing, Chris. Let me go in and see Yolanda again."

I was already pulling the truck out of the motel parking lot. "No, let's just go," I said. "You know what's going to happen if you go back there. Yolanda's just going to make some excuse about why she can't give you anything else."

Selena sighed and leaned her head back. "Yeah, you're right."

By the time we got back to our house, my dad had already arrived from San Antonio. We hung out for a while and made plans for the next day. Selena made a list of things for me to buy at the grocery store; she was planning to make my favorite meal of black-tipped shark.

Eventually, my dad went to the guest room to unpack. When he came back to the kitchen, Selena and I were paying bills. We both had our checkbooks out on the kitchen table. Seeing that made my dad laugh and get his camera.

"Here," he said, aiming the camera in our direction. "I want to get pictures of you two paying bills like grown-ups and being so responsible."

That was the very last picture ever taken of Selena alive.

If I had to pick my happiest memory with Selena, I'd probably pick the night before she was killed. Things were so good with us at that moment. As we always did, when Selena and I went to bed together, we hugged and said how much we loved each other. That night, she lay with her head on that sweet spot on my shoulder and we talked about the future. It was one of those moments when you're so in love with somebody and you feel that love coming back to you. I'm happy to have that memory of our last night together as a reminder of how rich and full of love our lives were, despite everything.

The phone rang as we were lying there, and Selena looked at me.

"What?" I said.

"It's Yolanda."

"How do you know?" I asked.

Selena rolled over and picked up the phone. After she'd said hello, Selena listened for a minute, then said to me, "Guess what? Yolanda found those missing papers. She wants me to come back to the motel and get them. She wants me to go alone."

"No!" I said. "Tell her that you're not going back. It's too late. No way. Plus, I don't want you going over there alone."

"No," Selena repeated into the phone. "Chris says it's too late. We'll come back tomorrow."

Yolanda then started talking about the rape. Selena stopped her and said, "If you want to go to the hospital, I'll take you. I already told you that."

When Yolanda said no, that she didn't want to go to the hospital, Selena said, "You know what? It's late, and this conversation is over." Then she hung up the phone.

"She probably thought I would be with you, and that's why she said no," I said.

"Yeah, and she probably also knows that if I take her to the hospital, they won't find anything wrong," Selena said. "Maybe I should go over there anyway."

"Don't. Just stay here with me," I said. "We'll handle everything tomorrow, okay?"

"Okay," Selena agreed, and we both fell asleep at last.

In the morning, I woke up to the sound of Selena shuffling things around in the bedroom. I opened one eye and watched her getting her clothes together. I didn't know where she was going, but I was too sleepy to wonder about it. I didn't even think about the motel or Yolanda.

Selena showered and dressed, then opened the door of our bedroom to leave. As she did, my dad opened the door to the guest bedroom at the same time. Selena had completely forgotten that he was in the house. She screamed at the sight of him—a really loud, scared kind of scream.

I jumped out of bed. "What? What's going on?" I shouted.

Selena turned around and started laughing that great big laugh of hers. "It's nothing. Go back to bed, Chris. I'm sorry. I forgot your dad was here. He really scared me!"

At the same time, I could see my dad in the hallway, apologizing. "I didn't mean to scare you," he said to Selena, but truthfully, he also looked pretty startled.

My dad and Selena talked for a few minutes in the hallway. I turned over and went back to sleep. I didn't even think to ask Selena why she was up so early. She often woke up before I did, got dressed, and chilled around the house, made phone calls, or went off to have breakfast with her dad. The only unusual thing about that morning was that I had been awakened by Selena screaming.

Selena, it turned out, was on her way to the Days Inn. She had talked to Yolanda again that morning, and she was determined to take Yolanda to the hospital and have her examined after the so-called rape. That was Selena's style: she was going to see this thing through and prove that Yolanda was lying.

Selena called me a little later that morning to tell me that she had taken Yolanda to Doctors Regional Hospital. Now they were returning to the Days Inn. "I couldn't find my keys," Selena confessed, "so I took your truck and your cell phone."

Yolanda was in the truck with her, so Selena lowered her voice as she told me that the doctors had found no evidence of rape.

There was nothing else Yolanda had now that could keep Selena there. They were on their way back to the motel and Selena would come home, I thought. Maybe we would finally be rid of that woman and her craziness.

I went with my dad in his car to pick up the groceries we needed for dinner and to run a few other errands. The sky was cloudy and gray, and the day had a gloomy feel to it.

Something made me decide to call off the other errands after we'd bought the groceries. "You know what?" I said to my dad. "Let's just go back to the house. I can go back out again later."

We left the seafood place where we'd bought the shark and drove home. When I saw that the answering machine light was blinking, I pushed PLAY and listened to a cryptic message from one of our DJ friends in the valley.

"Hey, Chris," he said. "Is everything okay? Call me back."

Why hadn't he called my cell phone? I wondered. Then I remembered that Selena had my phone in the truck with her. Nobody could reach me.

There was another message as well, this one from someone who had heard a rumor that Selena had been hurt or in an accident. I just rolled my eyes. Selena and I often got these kinds of crazy calls, because the media in Corpus was always looking for another story they could do about her.

I was in the bedroom and my dad was in the living room watching TV when the phone rang. I let the answering machine pick up the call. I never answered the phone right away.

This time, however, I heard Selena's aunt Dolores speaking and picked up the phone receiver immediately. "What's up?" I said.

Dolores sounded calm and fairly collected, but her voice was a little higher-pitched than usual, tight sounding. "Selena's been involved in an accident, Chris," she said, her voice starting to shake a little. "She's at Memorial Hospital. You need to get over there as soon as you can."

Immediately, I thought of how fast Selena liked to drive. *It must have been a car accident*, I thought. "What happened?" I asked, my heart starting to pound.

"Selena was shot twice," Aunt Dolores said. "You need to come to the hospital right away."

I hung up the phone, ran into the living room, and told my dad about the call. I was upset but still not panicked. People get shot and survive their wounds all of the time, I told myself.

By now, we were in the car. Aloud, I said to my dad, "Damn it, man, why did she have to go to that motel by herself this morning? Now look what's happened."

My dad had been going the speed limit. He began driving faster and faster the closer we got to Memorial Hospital. By the time he pulled into the hospital parking lot, he was driving so fast that the tires screeched as he went around that last corner.

In my mind, of course, Selena was still alive. I was going to go into that hospital and see her and hold her in my arms. The thought never entered my mind that my wife might not make it—much less that Selena might pass away before I could see her again.

Robert, one of our sound guys on the road, was already there; I saw him standing outside the main door smoking a cigarette, but he didn't say anything to me. My dad and I walked into the emergency room, and right away a bunch of doctors and nurses surrounded me. Somebody put a hand on my shoulder and said, "This way, son."

I was led into a waiting room. Everyone was already there: Abraham, Marcella, Suzette, and many other family members. Only A.B. was missing; he had already slipped away to grieve on his own.

When I saw them, I kind of gave everybody a smile, even though my stomach started twisting into knots at the sight of their expressions.

"What's going on?" I said. "Where's Selena?"

Abraham looked at me with dull eyes and said, "Selena passed away, Chris. She's dead. She was shot and she's dead."

For a moment, I stood there feeling stunned, absolutely numb from shock. How was it possible that I wasn't ever going to see my wife alive again? Never to kiss her or feel her arms around me?

Then I started sobbing, knowing that Selena was gone, but not really grasping it. It takes a while to believe that somebody is gone. You understand it, but you don't really believe it.

Abraham was crying, too, now. We didn't know all of the details of the shooting—those came out much later. Then everybody else started weeping with us, and I suddenly had to get out of that room, escape that wall of grief.

Selena's uncle Isaac, Abraham's younger brother, was sitting in the crowded waiting room, too. He must have seen how I was, for he opened the door and walked with me out into the hospital hallway. Two doctors were standing there. One of them said to me, "We're sorry for your loss. We did everything we could."

I couldn't speak. Then the doctors said, "We need you to come and identify the body."

"What?" I said, disbelieving, still, that any of this was happening. "What do you mean? What do I have to do?"

Isaac said, "What are you talking about? Selena's dead. Why does he have to look at her body?"

"Somebody needs to come and identify her," one of the doctors said gently. "It's standard procedure."

"I can't do that," I gasped. I felt like I might pass out from grief; I could scarcely breathe. All I could think about was how Selena had looked when she turned and laughed this morning in the bedroom and told me to go back to sleep. Selena was gone. How could she be gone?

"I'm sorry, but you have to come with us and identify her," the doctor was repeating.

I had been barely holding myself together. Now I went completely out of control, yelling at the doctors. "I can't do that right now, all right?" I shouted. "I told you that already. I just can't!"

Isaac stepped between me and the doctors and said, "What about me? Can I do it for him?"

"Are you a family member?" the doctor said.

"I'm her uncle," he said.

The doctors led him away, leaving me standing alone in the hallway, weeping.

My dad drove me home from the hospital. I don't know what time we left, or in what order anything happened. I was there, but not there. It was like a nightmare. I walked around the rooms and saw Selena's clothes on the bed and our paperwork still on the kitchen table from the night before. I walked into the bathroom, and there was Selena's robe, still draped over the shower rod from this morning. It occurred to me then that of course Selena hadn't known it would be her last day on this earth, either. I started to cry.

My family gathered at the house. Certain details were starting to emerge about the shooting and were slowly filtering into my numbed consciousness. I knew that Selena had gone to the Days Inn to meet Yolanda that morning, had taken her to the hospital and called me when they were on their way back to Yolanda's room. There had apparently been some kind of confrontation in the motel room—probably about the missing financial records—just before noon.

When Selena told Yolanda that she couldn't trust her anymore, Yolanda had drawn the gun from her purse. As Selena turned to leave the room, Yolanda had fired once into my wife's back, severing an artery to the heart.

Selena had managed to run across the parking lot toward the lobby, leaving a trail of blood and calling for help. She had collapsed on the lobby floor, soaked in blood, and begged the clerks to lock the door. She identified Yolanda as the shooter to one of the clerks, who then dialed an ambulance. The paramedics tried to stop Selena's internal bleeding and performed CPR; Selena was still alive when they arrived at Memorial Hospital. She had apparently taken off the ring that Yolanda had given her, because when one of the paramedics tried to find a vein for the IV, Selena's hand opened and the ring fell out.

In the hospital's trauma room, doctors and surgeons had tried blood transfusions after opening up her chest and discovering massive internal bleeding. Selena died at just after one o'clock in the afternoon. It was two days before our third wedding anniversary.

After shooting Selena, Yolanda had run to her truck and tried to flee the hotel parking lot, but the police had seen her trying to escape. Now, as our family gathered in the living room of our house, Yolanda was parked in her truck with the same pistol aimed at her right temple. She was threatening to kill herself.

I couldn't stay in the living room, watching the standoff as the police tried to negotiate and stop her from pulling the trigger. I didn't think that Yolanda would shoot herself. But I didn't really care what she did. It was as if I had been swallowed by a black cloud and couldn't see beyond my own grief.

I went into our bedroom to lie down. After a little while, I got up again and collected the clothes that Selena had been wearing the night before; she had left them on the floor beside the bed. My family was still watching the standoff with Yolanda on TV; in total, she would stay in that pickup truck outside the Days Inn for over nine hours before finally letting the police take her into custody.

Back in the bedroom, I sat on Selena's side of the bed and held her clothes. I could smell her perfume on them, and suddenly what I wanted more than anything else was to save that smell forever.

I returned to the kitchen and put Selena's clothes in a plastic bag so that I could seal in the smell. I had to walk by the living room; everyone looked up at me from the television where they were watching the standoff between the police and Yolanda.

"I don't know why you all are watching that," I told them. "She's not going to kill herself."

Yolanda kept saying that she was sorry for shooting Selena, but I didn't believe it. I was sure that she only wished that she had the nerve to pull that trigger, but she knew that she didn't, the same way that I knew it. This was all an act to show that she was feeling remorse. She wasn't: Yolanda was just sorry that she was caught.

I went back into our bedroom with Selena's clothes and held that bag in my arms, rocking a little on the edge of the bed.

For the longest time, I kept that bag of Selena's clothes. I would poke a hole in it now and then and squeeze the bag so that I could smell her perfume. Then I'd seal up the hole again as quickly as I could. I knew that I only had a certain number of times that I could do that before there would be nothing left of Selena.

FOURTEEN

RESURRECTION

*R*adio station KEDA-AM broke the news of Selena's death first. From there, the news traveled fast.

Mourners began arriving from all over. They drove, walked, and rode bicycles past our house on Bloomington Street, many stopping to create a shrine to Selena in front of our chain-link fence with balloons, colored ribbons, stuffed animals, drawings, photographs, scribbled notes, flowers, and flags from all over. At one point the line of cars wrapped around five blocks. Selena had been loved by everyone, from young children who loved to dance to "Bidi Bidi Bom Bom" to elderly Tejano fans. Now they were pouring out their love and grief.

The boutiques in Corpus Christi and San Antonio were transformed into shrines as well, and anguished fans held candlelight vigils around the country. Most of the cars in Corpus Christi drove with their headlights on. Fans also left notes and messages on the door of Room 158 of the Days Inn, where Selena was killed.

Selena's albums and cassettes rapidly disappeared from stores as Texas radio stations played her music nonstop. Grieving fans phoned the radio stations to read poetry for Selena on air, and other

Tejano artists shared their memories of her with the media. Mourners gathered in other cities around the world as well; in Los Angeles alone, four thousand people gathered at the Sports Arena Memorial to honor Selena.

The mourners continued to stand outside our house for months after Selena's death, sometimes even at night. They were in the street all of the time. It didn't matter. I didn't want to go out anyway.

The night before Selena's funeral, we held a viewing for family and close friends at the funeral home. I hadn't yet seen Selena's body. I sat in the front row maybe ten feet away from the casket, unable to look anywhere but at a spot on the floor maybe a foot in front of my feet. I sat there with her family, just staring at that spot, feeling Selena close but not able to look at her, much less approach the casket. I was paralyzed by grief.

"Come on, Chris," everyone urged me. "You need to say good-bye."

"Man, I don't want to do that," I told them. "I can't see her like this."

Everything felt surreal, and the whole business at the funeral home, which was packed with people, with many more lined up outside all night to get inside, felt like a spectacle to me. I hadn't had any time alone with Selena.

I was clutching the ring I had bought for Selena to celebrate our second wedding anniversary, the ring I'd hidden in her pillowcase in Jamaica. I had it on one of my fingers and I kept twiddling it around in my hand.

Selena's family, meanwhile, did a wonderful job of talking to people who came to pay their respects. When the viewing hours were over, her uncle Isaac came over to me and said, "Chris, you haven't gone up to see her. Why not?"

I was crying. "I can't," I said. "I can't go up there and see her."

"Come on," he said gently, and then Isaac literally picked me up off the chair by hooking an arm around my shoulders.

I didn't resist. As we walked to the casket, though, my legs started shaking so badly that I nearly collapsed. I hadn't eaten anything in two days and my clothes were already falling off my body.

"You know what," Isaac said. "Stop right here for a minute. I'm going to get everybody out of the room. It's going to be just you and her, son."

I halted next to him. I couldn't have gone anywhere without his support anyway. Just as he'd promised, Isaac announced, "Everybody out, please. We need privacy here."

He led me up to the casket once the room was cleared and left me there. Once everybody else was gone, I felt, okay, the show was over.

"It's just you and me now," I whispered to my wife.

I stood there crying and looking at her for a minute. Then I gave Selena a kiss on the forehead and stroked her hand. She looked so comfortable and peaceful lying there in the coffin that I just wanted to get in there with her and lie down beside her, put my arm around her, close the top, and say, "Let's go."

After a few minutes, though, I got the ring out of my pocket and put it on Selena's wedding ring finger. Then I got down on my knees right there and said a prayer, the tears still streaming down my face, and said my last good-bye.

The next day, we held Selena's funeral at Seaside Memorial Park in Corpus Christi. My friend Rudy drove me there in his car. I don't remember much of that day, other than the thick gray clouds gathered overhead and being aware of wearing my wedding ring. I was in too much of a daze to notice much beyond my small circle of pain. I had already said good-bye the night before at the funeral home, so at the actual cemetery there was really nothing left inside me. I was just a shell.

I heard later that more than sixty thousand people attended, and celebrities like Celia Cruz, Madonna, Julio Iglesias, and Gloria Estefan sent their condolences. Her fans lined up along Shoreline Boulevard for almost a mile to view Selena's casket on the way to the service at Bayfront Auditorium. We had surrounded Selena's closed casket with five thousand white roses, her favorite flower. We also asked those attending the funeral service to place white roses on the coffin. By the time Selena was buried, a two-foot pile of roses was piled on top of the coffin.

Selena's death had such a widespread impact that news about it ran on the front page of *The New York Times* for two days running.

On April 12, 1995, two weeks after Selena's death, then-Governor George W. Bush declared her birthday "Selena Day" in Texas. Selena was also entered into *Billboard*'s International Latin Music Hall of Fame.

I was oblivious to all of this. I was barely conscious, imprisoned inside the walls of my own grief. A big part of me had died with Selena. I was, for all practical purposes, dead myself after we buried her.

I would have given anything to have her back.

Somehow, I made it through the trial that October. The jury deliberated for only two hours before finding Yolanda guilty of murder and sentencing her to life in prison for murder with a deadly weapon. The trial judge ordered that the .38 pistol Yolanda used to shoot Selena be chopped into fifty pieces that were scattered across the bay in Corpus Christi.

From her cell in the Mountain View Unit in Gatesville, Yolanda continued to maintain that she was innocent, saying that the shooting was an accident. She also tried to spread rumors about Selena and her family about everything imaginable—and about many things that weren't. No one ever uncovered any evidence to support her ugly rumors.

I paid no attention. I was still numb and didn't care about any of it. I was dimly aware of being glad that Yolanda had gotten life in prison. Death would have been too easy for her, and she deserved to have to live with what she had done. The justice system had done what it could. No verdict could change the fact that Selena was gone. Meanwhile, I continued to live, though many wouldn't have called it that.

I stayed on in our house in Corpus for a while. I wanted to surround myself with Selena's family, with her belongings and our dogs, with anything that could help me keep Selena close. The hardest thing was going to bed at night. Selena and I had a king-size bed; it was so big that sometimes I'd wake up and joke around when I saw her on the other side of the mattress, waving at her like we were standing across a river from each other. Selena would wave back. Now, when I woke up, I was alone on one side of the river. She had crossed it but I couldn't see her.

I shut myself off from everything. I didn't want to go anywhere, do anything, or see anybody. I was just trying to be. There were periods when I slept a lot and other times when I stayed up for three days straight. I started to drink heavily.

The months crawled by. People kept trying to pull me out of my well of grief. Nothing worked. I slept with pictures of Selena, snapshots of her doing ordinary, everyday things, like dusting or playing with the dogs, because that's how I saw her. I even carried stacks of photos around with me, so that I'd have her with me everywhere I went. I'd go to a friend's house, maybe, and be surrounded by well-meaning people, but I'd still be that weird guy sitting alone, off in a corner with my pictures of Selena. I ached for her every day.

Occasionally, Abraham would insist that I come over to Q Productions. He, A.B., and Suzette all went back to work, coping with the murder of their beloved daughter and sister in their own ways. They were trying to keep Selena's memory alive and hoping to bring me along with them into a future where I no longer felt like I had a place. Why would I want to live in a world without Selena?

Whenever I did make that rare appearance at Q Productions, I would walk in and hear a gasp from Selena's aunt Dolores, who worked at the front desk. Dolores scarcely recognized me anymore. I was so thin that my pants didn't fit and my shirts were just barely hanging on my body. People kept trying to make me eat lunch or dinner with them, but I'd always say that I wasn't hungry. That was the truth, too.

My mother visited regularly. She was trying to help me rejoin the living any way she could: talking to me, cooking, cleaning the house. One day, she was scrubbing out our bathroom when I heard something crash to the floor.

I snapped out of my stupor and ran to her. "Mom? You okay?"

She was standing in the bathroom with a hand over her mouth, staring at a pill bottle on the floor. It was a bottle of folic acid tablets—pills that women take during pregnancy. My mother looked at me, a question in her eyes.

"I know what you're thinking, but no, Mom," I said gently. "Selena wasn't pregnant. She took these pills for a while because she'd heard that folic acid is good for your hair."

The truth was that Selena and I had been talking about having children just before she died. Once the mainstream album was released, once we had promoted it and played some shows, we had decided it was time to move forward with our own family.

If Selena had lived, would she have become the next Gloria Estefan, conquering the pop charts? I thought so, but in a way it didn't matter. Selena and I already had each other. We were ready to build our dream house on those ten beautiful acres of land in Corpus and get started on the next chapter of our lives.

Now I was thankful that at least Selena wasn't pregnant, and that I hadn't lost my child as well as my wife.

After about six months, Selena's death no longer felt like that constant, piercing pain. Instead I had an empty, hollow, sad feeling that I imagined would never go away, punctuated by silent howls of despair when something reminded me on a deeper level that Selena was really gone—like when I picked up the phone to call her, and realized how much I missed hearing her voice. I tried to dull my emotions with drugs and alcohol, slipping further out of the life that seemed so pointless now.

Occasionally, though, I began to have moments when I'd force my grief into a corner and try to start over. "She wouldn't want you to do this," I'd remind myself. "You have to keep on living for her."

When I could, I wrote a little music and lost myself in my guitar. Somehow this was possible: I could express my grief through music, when words just wouldn't do it.

Around this time, I met a charismatic, talented singer named John Garza who became my friend and, in many ways, my protector during my darkest times. John moved into my house and made sure that I made it home in one piece each night no matter what I did to escape the body that trapped my soul inside it, preventing me from joining Selena.

John and I started working on music together, just a little bit here and there. I admired John's voice, because whenever he sang, it seemed as if he could convey the rush of feelings behind the words I was writing.

John didn't know me before Selena passed. He saw the crazy lifestyle that I was leading, but to his credit, he never judged me or made me feel bad about the things I was doing to myself. He understood what I was going through and simply watched my back as I struggled to find some meaning in my life again, even though I was looking for that meaning in all the wrong places.

Once, John and I found ourselves in a hotel in San Antonio. I was preoccupied with some football game that was about to start. We didn't have any alcohol, so I said, "Dude, I'm going to run out and get some beer real quick."

We took off from the hotel. I was in a hurry because I didn't want to miss the kickoff. I started jogging across the parking lot, John maintaining a steady pace beside me.

All of a sudden, I realized that my mouth was moving but no

sound was coming out. I knew that I was talking. Yet, I couldn't hear anything but this incredibly noisy wind in my ears, or maybe it was inside my head.

I stopped running and froze in place. John stopped beside me. "What's wrong?" he asked.

"My heart stopped," I said.

John put his hand on my chest. There was nothing, he said. No sound. Then, suddenly, "boom boom," my heart started beating again and my hearing returned.

I went right on over to the liquor store and bought some beer. That's the state of mind I was in.

Selena's mainstream album, *Dreaming of You*, was released in the summer of 1995. The album combined songs in both Spanish and English. It was Selena's biggest musical success yet, debuting at number one on the U.S. *Billboard* 200 chart—the first time for any Hispanic singer. The album sold over 175,000 copies on its release date, a record for any commercial woman singer, and it sold two million copies in one year alone.

I heard songs from that album everywhere I went, and it was torture. Anytime I heard Selena's voice come on the radio, I had to change the station. If I heard one of the songs in a restaurant, I wouldn't want to make a scene by walking out, but I'd pretend not to hear it. I got really good at just sitting there and acting like I couldn't hear any music at all.

Watching the music video for "I Could Fall in Love," one of the hit tracks from that album, was even worse. It was like slashing the wounds open all over again.

It took me over a year to really begin clawing my way out of that trench of despair. For a long time, I had kept everything in the house just the way it was, including Selena's belongings, but little by little I started putting a few things away. Some days, walking by them made me feel good, because I had such fond, loving memories of Selena. Other times, though, I would see something of hers and sink into a depression that lasted for days, consumed as I was by grief. I had to find a way to move on.

With John, I decided to finally pursue a dream that would have made Selena proud: I formed a rock band that included my old friend and former La Mafia member Rudy Martinez on bass; Joe Ojeda, who had played keyboards with us in Los Dinos; and Jesse Esquivel on drums.

Abraham and A.B. would probably have helped me out with producing, but I decided that I needed to make the album independently. I was finally going to try to create the record that I had been hearing in my head, and I was determined to work with people who could get me that sound. I put the band together. In 1998, the Chris Perez Band—not my idea to name it that, but the guys insisted—went to Los Angeles to record our music at Henson Studio.

The most unlikely song on the album was one that I had written about Selena a few months earlier. Called "Best I Can," that song cataloged a lot of the despair I was feeling and my struggle to go on.

I remember that I was sitting alone in the living room when I wrote it, barefoot and in my sweats. It was during that time of day that Selena loved so much, when the sun was setting and it hit a certain spot on our living room floor. We always put our feet in that spot of sunlight to warm them.

I picked up my guitar and the music just flowed out of my fingers. Part of me knew that it was a good song, but another part of me didn't want anyone else to hear it. I was reluctant to reveal my emotions to the world, much less use my personal tragedy to sell a record. It was bad enough to be known as "the widower of the slain Queen of Tejano Music," or whatever the media was calling me. I didn't want to also have to hear people saying, "Yeah, well, that record got made only because he wrote about Selena. He's just pulling on heartstrings by putting that one out."

When I finished writing the song, I felt okay but bad at the same time. I was split in two; great songs deserve to be heard, but this one would be mine alone.

I put down my guitar and then started writing the lyrics. Those, too, came out fully formed, which is rare—not just for me, but for any songwriter. Usually I have to sit and think about a song before I can start writing, then rewrite the lyrics over and over again until they seem perfect. With this song, however, it was as if Selena's spirit was there to guide me as I wrote,

I can't erase this lonely heart that keeps on remembering.
Every day I live, I live with you, and with all the things
we'll never do.
Heaven holds a place for souls like mine.
Try to leave my troubled past behind.
You know it's so damn hard letting go . . .
Standing here, holding my heart in my hands
Yes, I am . . .
Trying to live every day the best I can.

After I'd finished writing "Best I Can," I worked on the music for another of our songs, "Solo Tu." Joe had written the words and left them on a sheet of paper on my mixing board. He had been thinking of turning it into a romantic ballad, but I picked it up and decided to make it into a rock song.

By the time John and Joe came over that night, I had two songs to show them. I played "Solo Tu" for them first, and we worked on that one together for a while.

Then I said, "I also wrote this other thing. But, before I show it to you, I want you to know that I don't want to ever put this song out." I got out the lyrics, sat down with my guitar, and started playing "Best I Can."

"Wow," they both said when I finished. "We've got to at least do a demo, even if you don't want to release it."

So we recorded "Best I Can" with studio gear, but with no intention of including it on the album. When we arrived in Los Angeles and started recording, however, I was outvoted by the other band members and by the people at our label, Hollywood Records, who had accidentally heard the demo and loved that song more than any other. Together, they all managed to talk me into it.

"Selena always supported you one hundred percent," Joe said. "She would love it that you wrote this song for her, and that you're going ahead with your dream to have a rock band."

There was another song about Selena on the album called "Another Day." I don't know why I was cool with sharing that song, but not "Best I Can," especially since "Another Day" was about how much I loved Selena. It was just one of those personal, maybe irrational, feelings.

The thing is, making music has never been about making money for me. I had never tried to see the road in front of me. I just wanted to write songs that people could hear and relate to their own experiences, whatever situations they're going through. I ended up deciding to release "Best I Can" not only because it was a good song and the other band members wanted it on the album, but because I thought that hearing it might help others who had lost loved ones. That's what music has always been about for me, as it was for Selena: connecting with other people in ways that you can't through words alone.

It took us a couple of months to record the CD. In the final production, I ended up working with another childhood friend, bass guitarist Adriel Ramirez, and drummer Alex Tamez, as well as with my friends John and Joe. I also brought in musicians from other genres to conquer the unique sounds I was after. These included percussionist Luis Conte, horn players from the Voodoo Glow Skulls, Mariachi Sol de Mexico, and even members of the band Cheap Trick. If we succeeded in the U.S. rock market, I knew we'd be conquering new territory as U.S.-born, Latin musicians.

When *Resurrection* was released in 1999, it included nine tracks in Spanish and six in English. I wanted this Latin rock album to break new cultural ground, in the sense that its bilingual mix reflected the daily reality for many Hispanic-Americans who were growing up the way Selena and I had.

In a bold move, our label released two different singles at the same time to both English and Spanish radio stations: the rock song "Resurrection" as the first English-language single, and "Por Que Te Fuiste," a ballad that I knew would appeal to Spanish-speaking listeners. I started going to different radio stations and working with promoters in the U.S. and abroad. Oddly, hitting the road to do the interviews and shows brought me closer to Selena, because now I was experiencing that life again. What's more, because the Chris Perez Band carried my name, and because I had written or cowritten nine of the songs on the album, I was the one the media was interested in now.

Anytime I felt tired or irritable from marketing the music, I would remember how Selena would get up every day and do whatever it took to help her family, support and love me, care for our house, reach out to fans, and bring her music to the world. I never fully realized how much Selena was juggling, or how much courage she had, until I started going on the road and revealing my own vulnerabilities in the music I was writing.

I used to say to her, "Just ignore what people say. There's always going to be some negativity, and you can't worry about it or take it personally." Now that I was feeling the sting of negative remarks sometimes, I realized how tough and determined Selena truly was. I vowed not to let her down.

Our album was aptly named: this was my personal resurrection, I decided. I would live and work in a way that made Selena proud of me from now on.

A few months after I'd returned from the promotional tour for *Resurrection*, I got a call early one morning from my friend Robert Trevino, who works for Gibson Guitars. "Congratulations, Chris!" he said.

"Dude, do you know what time it is?" I said, blinking hard at the clock.

"Yeah, but I wanted to be the first one to congratulate you."

"For what?" I asked. "What are you talking about?"

"You're nominated for a Grammy," Robert said.

"Shut up," I said. "Somebody told me you can't be nominated for a Grammy until you've got three or four CDs. That's impossible."

"Oh, man, sorry," he said. "I guess I screwed up."

"Where did you hear this, anyway?" I asked.

"I'm on the Web site. The nominations came out today," Robert said.

"Well, you must have read it wrong," I said.

We hung up, but of course I had to go and check it out for myself. Sure enough, there was my name on the list. I called Robert right back to apologize. "You're right! We were nominated!"

He laughed. "I told you, *pendejo.*"

"Yeah, well. It doesn't matter, because look who we're up against," I reminded him. "We're never going to win. Still, it's an honor to be nominated, right?"

I called everyone in the band and told them the news. We decided to fly out to Los Angeles for the ceremony and just watch the show and enjoy the ride.

When we walked into the theater, I saw A.B. and his bandmate, Cruz Martinez. They were dressed up in these weird outfits. I'd worn background clothes, a nice suit, and I'd brought my whole band. When I saw A.B. dressed like that, along with all of these other artists whose music I admired so much, I suddenly felt like I shouldn't be there at all. Whoever nominated us must have made a mistake. These other people had put out lots of albums; I hadn't worked nearly hard enough yet to deserve this honor.

But we were here, so I said hello to A.B. and then went to my seat. I was seated near the stage and A.B. was sitting up in the bleachers on the side. As I looked at him, I wondered if A.B. was remembering, like I was, Selena's Grammy award and her speech that night.

I wondered if Selena was watching us right now. I hoped that she was. I knew this would make her so proud to see both her brother and me in these seats. She'd be laughing that laugh of hers, too, if she saw how nervous I was.

"You see how it feels?" I could imagine her saying. "At least you don't have to worry about tripping on your dress!"

My category came up first. When the MCs started listing the nominees for Best Latin Rock Alternative Performance for 1999, of course I knew that my band wasn't going to win. These other musicians were so great, so artistic, and I owned CDs by every one of them because I loved their music so much. It was a pretty safe bet that they couldn't say the same thing about my CD. They probably didn't even know who I was.

Then they opened the envelope, and said, "The winner is . . ."

In my head, I heard Cafe Tacuba's *Reves Yo Soy*. I loved that album and knew they deserved the award.

I was getting ready to stand up and clap for that cool badass band, Cafe Tacuba, when, in my peripheral vision, I saw John jump up. I looked over and saw the other guys in my band standing up as well. I was still sitting down. Then they all started clapping and gesturing for me to go on up to the stage.

"We won, man, we won!" John said.

I stood up and took my walk to the podium, knowing that, if she could see me now, Selena would be smiling.

In the end, all I did was make the best record I could with friends and musicians I admired. I never thought we'd win a

Grammy, but as Selena always told the children she spoke to around the country, "Nothing is impossible if you work hard."

That includes picking up the pieces of your life.

Selena has continued to have a profound impact on the world. *Dreaming of You* was listed as one of the bestselling records of 1995 by *Billboard* magazine. That jump into the top slot made Selena one of the bestselling women musical artists in history; only Janet Jackson had done better at that point in time. After the album's release, the songs "I Could Fall in Love" and "Dreaming of You" topped the charts worldwide as well.

In her honor, Selena's family established the Selena Foundation, a charitable organization with the mission of helping children in crisis, the poor, and the elderly. The foundation raises money through donations and the sale of Selena albums and items from Q Productions, which also operates the Selena Museum in Corpus Christi. Thousands of people still travel to Corpus Christi from all over the U.S. and Latin America each year to visit the museum, Selena's grave, and our old home.

On March 27, 1997, the movie *Selena* was released. Directed by Gregory Nava and starring Jennifer Lopez as Selena and Jon Seda in my role, the movie introduced a new generation of fans to Selena's life and music. Six years later, we held a tribute concert in Houston's Reliant Stadium called *Selena Vive*, asking stars like Gloria Estefan, Thalia, Soraya, and other Latin performers to play Selena's music as a tribute to her and to the more than sixty-five thousand people who attended. The show was recorded for television and became one of the most-viewed Spanish-language TV shows in the

U.S. And, on March 16, 2011, the United States Post Office released a "Latin Legends" stamp in memory of Selena and other Latin music greats, like Tito Puente and Celia Cruz.

My life has gone on. More than anything, I am grateful to Selena for teaching me the meaning of love. I was fortunate enough to be able to marry again and have children. I wish that I could have had a family with Selena, as we had always planned; still, I know that Selena was the one who made this possible for me. She showed me how to drop my guard and embrace life.

I used to talk on the phone with my family frequently, but it wasn't until I married Selena that I truly opened my heart. Today I say "I love you" to my friends and family every chance I get, because I know that there might not be another tomorrow with these people who are so dear to me. I know that, if Selena were here, she'd tell me that she loved me and not to worry, because I'll see her again one day.

Selena inspired me and she inspired the world. She provided her fans with everything they needed, from dance tunes to soulful ballads. Through her own life and through her music, Selena showed those who were struggling—migrant workers, schoolchildren, housewives with domineering husbands, teens rebelling against their conservative parents—that persistence and hard work pay off, and that you can be ambitious without leaving your family or cherished values behind. This message especially resonated with Hispanic-Americans, many of whom, like Abraham, had experienced racism during their lives simply for speaking Spanish—or just looking like they could.

Selena's fans felt like they knew her because she opened her heart to the world and let herself be known. She was one of us, one of ours, and we felt like Selena was always going to be here. We watched her grow up and saw her star rise. Selena represented the idea that it is possible to go places that most of us only dream about.

Selena, I'm still dreaming of you.

ACKNOWLEDGMENTS

Jeff Silberman—for answering all my questions about how to go about writing a book and helping me see this project through from the beginning to the end.

Holly Robinson—for taking the time to listen to my stories and helping to put them down on paper.

Pete Salgado—for believing in me, my music, and this book. I could not have finished this without your help.

Peter Paterno—for all the years of believing in me and all your hard work. Thank you.

Thanks to my loving and supportive family:

Mom, Dad, Pop, Chuck and Pati, Melissa, Moses (Uncle Nuni) and the Vara Family, Uncle Lee and Mary Ann (Memen) Johnson, Rosemary Vara, Tia Toni Perez Mencey, cousins Kenney and Janie Mencey, Phillip "Chacho" Mishoe, Michael Perez, Bill Mishoe, Shane and Monica Pulver, Stephanie Sanchez.

Thanks to my friends (my other family):

Jesse J. Oliva (Rest in Peace, bro. We miss you.), Rudy Martinez, Carlos Miranda Jr., *la familia* Espinosa-Carrillo. Horacio, Maria, and Amanda Jiménez. Robert "Bobbo" Gomez and the entire Gomez Clan, John Z. Garza, John J. Silva, Victor Flores, Gilbert Vela, Jon Seda, Robert Treviño (Gibson Guitars LN), Angel Ferrer.

Special thanks to:

The Quintanilla family—Abraham, Marcella, A.B., Suzette Quintanilla Arriaga, Billy Arriaga, Jovan Arriaga, Martika and S'vani Quintanilla.

Los Dinos—Ricky Vela, Joe Ojeda, Pete Astudillo. Thank you, guys.

Carlos Valdez, Mark Skurka and the prosecution's entire legal team—Thank you all so much for your hard work and dedication in making sure that justice for Selena was served.

Finally, I would like to save my biggest thanks for Cassie and Noah Perez. You two kids are the brightest lights in my life. Daddy loves you more than anything.